PRAISE FOR SUCCESS BY THE NUMBERS

"In *Success by the Numbers*, Marcia pierces through the fog of confusion by giving entrepreneurs a step-by-step process to follow by brilliantly using the art and science of numerology. A must-read for any entrepreneur who wants clarity both about what they do and about how to lead a visionary business today."
Janet Bray Attwood – New York Times Author, The Passion Test -The Effortless Path To Discovering Your Life Purpose

"Recognized as a pioneer in the coaching industry for decades, once again Marcia Bench accomplishes this recognition in the entrepreneurial space with her latest work, *Success by the Numbers*. Taking the complex topic of numerology from the fringes of society to mainstream, Marcia unequivocally proves how this ancient study is highly applicable to today's entrepreneurial success. Experts and entrepreneurs from virtually every industry will benefit from the information in *Success by the Numbers*. Bench's writing style is engaging, entertaining and easy to understand. Readers will be in awe of how incredibly accurate the information is as it pertains to their business success. A must read."
Kathleen Gage, Online Marketing Strategist and author of 101 Ways to Get Your Foot in the Door

"Marcia Bench took the study of numerology and applied it against all aspects of your life, including your business. As I did my calculations it is fascinating to discover the likeness to everything that I was to my number. Even more amazing was my business translated to everything we do and are doing. It was like verifying destiny with a few simple calculations. It's an incredibly insightful book, and may even answer some questions about why you do what you do, why you like what you like, and where your business is headed."
Tracy Repchuk, Internet Marketing and Social Media Strategist and Speaker, Best-Selling Author of 31 Days to Millionaire Marketing Miracles

"*Success by the Numbers* is a powerful book for any coach wanting

to create massive success in their business! Marcia's application of numerology principles to the business world provides deep insights and practical ways to move you toward your goals."
Christian Mickelsen, CoachesWithClients.com

"Extraordinary! This book gives you a fascinating key -- your

personalized numerical code -- that unlocks the secret to living your life on purpose, with passion and profitability. Definitely a 'must-have' guide that you'll refer to again and again!"
Kendall SummerHawk, Leading Expert in Women Entrepreneurs and Money, Co-founder of the International Association of Women in Coaching

"*Success by the Numbers* is a delightful way to explore numerology as

it relates to your business, career, and life path. Certainly any method that helps us get more clarity about our talents and abilities assists us in expanding what we believe about our possibilities in this lifetime. It's really quite fascinating and enlightening, and I encourage you to pick up a copy of Marcia's book, do the exercises and see for yourself!"
Dr. Sheri Rosenthal, author of The Complete Idiot's Guide to Toltec Wisdom and Banish Mind Spam!

"With this groundbreaking book, Marcia Bench has done it again.

Who knew that numerology could offer such amazing spiritual insights that lead directly to business success! I recommend you read it from cover to cover and apply its principles in your business."
Eva Gregory, Chief Fun Officer, Leading Edge Coaching & Training

"Marcia Bench certainly knows how to make the numbers work--

her remarkable talent shines in all that she has created during more than 25 years of professional excellence and through authoring 25 transformational books. *Success by the Numbers* is her best yet! I highly recommend this comprehensive guide to getting all the numbers working for you and your business."
Viki Winterton, Founder and Publisher, Expert Insights Publishing

"I'm always inspired by Marcia Bench and her deep commitment to

connecting spiritual tools with business success. If you're leading a visionary life, you'll want to discover the power of applying ancient wisdom to today's world. Well-researched, presented and highly relevant. Thanks Marcia!"
Rev. Karen Russo, MBA, award-winning author, The Money Keys

"As a professional speaker and long-time business owner, I'm always

looking for new tools that shed light on my business and that of my clients. This amazing book does just that - it's clear, concise, and yet reveals information I've never read anywhere else. I recommend it to any beginning or seasoned entrepreneur!"
Debbie Allen, International Business and Brand Strategist and Professional Speaker

SUCCESS
by the
NUMBERS:

DISCOVER YOUR KEYS TO WEALTH AND FULFILLMENT THROUGH BUSINESS NUMEROLOGY

Marcia Bench

This publication is designed to provide accurate and authoritative information in regard to the subject matter covered. It is sold with the understanding that the publisher is not engaged in rendering professional services. If legal, accounting, medical, psychological, or any other expert assistance is required, the services of a competent professional person should be sought. Client names have been changed to protect identities.

Library of Congress Cataloging-in-Publication Data:

Bench, Marcia

Success by the Numbers: Discover Your Keys to Wealth and Fulfillment through Business Numerology

/ Marcia Bench

      1. Spirituality 2. Entrepreneurship 3. Business 4. Work/ Career

ISBN 978-0-9817005-9-5

Printed in the United States of America

"Success by the Numbers: Discover Your Keys to Wealth and Fulfillment through Business Numerology"

TABLE OF CONTENTS

PART THREE: THE "OTHER NUMBERS" THAT MAKE YOU UNIQUE

PART FOUR: COMMON BARRIERS TO SUCCESS

PART FIVE: DOING BUSINESS BY THE NUMBERS

PART SIX: THE RHYTHM OF YOUR SUCCESS

ACKNOWLEDGEMENTS

Although it is the author that brings the words and concepts to paper in any book or similar endeavor, none of us ever does it alone. I am grateful to the friends who first introduced me to numerology in my early 20's, as well as my instructors Alison Baughman and others, and the other authors of books on numerology, who shared the magic of numerology with me.

I am also grateful to my coach and friend, Kathleen Gage, and my fellow Mastermind colleagues, for encouraging me to pursue this path despite it being a seeming departure from my past work as a business coach, trainer and author. The spiritual part of my life and work (expressing itself as numerology now) has always been present – it is just taking on a place of greater significance the further I go along the pathway.

I thank the many business coaches and mentors I have had over the years, the dynamic speakers and authors who have shared their wisdom with me, and my clients and students who are always awakening me to deeper meanings and new truths in the "tried and true" principles that undergird my work.

And I thank the Universal Presence, God, the Ultimate Inspiration, for allowing me the honor to take form in this body at this amazing time in our history, and to share the gifts and talents I have been given to help so many others do the same. Namaste.

INTRODUCTION

What you are holding in your hands is a guidebook to your future – to fulfillment, success, and abundance unlike any you have known before. We human beings are designed as multisensory beings for a reason. While our mind is useful to learn concepts, and our physical senses to implement those concepts, our intuition and spiritual perception are also required for us to live fully. Haven't you had times when you had a "gut instinct" that something wasn't right – but you did it anyway? We all have! The source of that instinct is your deeper self, your Higher Self, the infinite part of you that knows without thinking, decides without analyzing, and guides you to your greatness.

Numerology, in essence, is the study of the energy of numbers – especially those revealed in your birth date and birth name – as a lens to access your soul's ultimate agenda for your life. It in turn gives you more tangible access to your intuition and spiritual gifts so that you can use them effectively in a job, career or business to realize true inner (and outer) success. I first discovered it through a friend when I was in my 20's, and the amazing insights it gave stuck with me (though I didn't study it at that time).

Then just a few years ago, after more than 25 years of work with entrepreneurs and professionals, helping them hone their brand, market their services, develop their web site and enroll clients, the thought kept coming to me to look more deeply into numerology. And knowing my intuitive nudges as I do, I followed the thought!

That led to me studying the work of the other experts in the field and becoming certified through two different programs – still not knowing exactly what I was going to do with it. And the more I studied, the more I realized: no one else was adequately addressing how to use numerology in your work or business, to discover the type of work or business that is ideal for you, and to align with the best timing — as revealed in numerology — to start a business, launch a product, change jobs or downsize.

Earlier in my career I pioneered an entire industry with my work on career coaching — creating the leading textbook in that field and the first and leading worldwide coach training organization with that specialty. And I believe that this book announces the birth of another new industry: Business Numerology! My company, Your Divine Gifts, now teaches live and online classes and live seminar events, offers readings and does coaching in how to apply numerology to your business or profession, and also offers the first ever certification as a Certified Business Numerologist. (See the back of this book or our web site at www.yourdivinegifts.com for more information on our various offerings.)

HOW THE BOOK IS ORGANIZED

I have organized the book so that it can be used both as a primer on numerology — to help you become familiar with what it can tell you and how it can be used — as well as an ongoing reference whenever you have a decision to make, are facing changes in your career or business, or things aren't flowing and you want to find out why.

Part One provides you with an orientation to what numerology is, how it applies to business, and how to calculate the two key numbers that comprise your Inspired Success Path.

Part Two gives you a detailed description of each of the 9 basic Inspired Success Paths and the 2 Master Success Paths so that you can better understand your own soul's agenda — and that of others close to you in your life and work. Each Inspired Success Paths represents a cluster of traits and experiences that your soul has chosen to play with in this lifetime, and which are critical to understand for you to gain the most value and make the right decisions for you regarding your chosen work or business direction. It also helps you understand the reasons for some of the challenges you may be facing so that you can either change course or at least reconcile yourself to these reasons and navigate them with more ease.

Part Three helps you understand four other numbers that are also important to understanding yourself and any differences between your inner and outer selves. You will also understand the reasons behind mid-life career and life changes with what you learn in Chapter 17.

Part Four demystifies common barriers to success including so-called "karma" in your profile, blocks in your energy system (or "chakras"), and sabotaging or outdated beliefs. Knowing what these blocks are and how to clear them can do wonders for your professional progress!

Part Five shows you how to use numerology to choose your business name, product name, and key dates (such as your start-up date or a merger date) to lean the odds in favor of success. It also teaches you how to identify and leverage your "zone of excellence" and choose your ideal market using numerology, as well as your staff.

Part Six shows you how to use the forecasting or timing elements of numerology both for goal-setting and planning as well as to understand and better accept the slower times in the cycles of activity (in business and life).

I recommend that you read chapters 1 and 2 in detail first, read the chapter in Part Two that corresponds to your Inspired Success Path, and then read Parts Three, Four, Five and Six to broaden your understanding of how to apply your Inspired Success Path at work. Then, you may wish to calculate the Inspired Success Path for business partners, staff, family members or friends and read the chapters pertaining to their Path to make your relationship closer or more effective (depending on whether it is a business or personal connection).

I can't wait to share this information with you, and to hear how you apply it in your work or business! Do contact me at www. yourdivinegifts.com with your comments, ok? Here's to your wealth, success and fulfillment "by the numbers"!

--Marcia Bench

PART ONE:

HOW THE NUMBERS REVEAL YOUR INSPIRED SUCCESS PATH

In this Part, we will explore the basics of Business Numerology, including:

- What numerology is – and its origins
- How numerology can help you increase your success
- How to calculate your Inspired Success Path

1

THE NUMEROLOGY/ SUCCESS CONNECTION

Did you know that the keys to your success – your optimal path in life and work – is revealed through the ancient science of numerology? It's amazing to discover that by using just two simple pieces of information about you – your name and your birth date – you can gain the insights you need to stop guessing, wishing and hoping that your business or career focus is right...and instead know what is best for you! You can also learn to time your career and business activities (start-up, staff additions, job changes, mergers and more) through Business Numerology.

For example: since I was a little girl, I have felt driven to achieve and excel – to be the best. Whether it was being the winner at card games, graduating at the top of my class, leading music at church, teaching Sunday school, or starting my own business at a young age, leadership came naturally to me. In addition, I was always curious about how things fit together - not mechanically, but conceptually: what are the rules here (in the company, in the family, and in life)? Why do you do it this way and not that way? And how could it be designed to have both desired outcomes instead of having to choose?

All the assessment tools I took in school – and later when I studied psychology and coaching – all encouraged me to pursue fields where I could exercise these talents. But I never understood why I was drawn to these areas – until I discovered numerology. I began to understand that even before I took my first breath, my soul had decided what natural gifts and talents I would bring into this lifetime, what areas of growth and opportunity I would seek to master, the challenges I would have and the optimal timing for all of this to occur. I had just forgotten what it was!

Your soul also has an agenda for this lifetime. It is not destiny or fate – in the sense that you have no choice whether or not to follow it. But knowing what it is – as you will discover in this book – can help you both align your life and work direction with that plan so that things flow better in your life, as well as understand the setbacks and adversity that is the inevitable part of anyone's life.

I was exposed to numerology years ago, but it was only recently – after decades of working as a workshop leader, teacher, coach, consultant and speaker, working with entrepreneurs as well as professionals and companies – that I became a Certified Numerologist. And it was amazing how many ways I began to see that numerology could be applied to work, to business, and to success. But when I began researching the topic of Business Numerology – reading virtually every book on numerology on the market – I found that most spent only a couple of pages addressing the subject as it relates to business success. So I set about addressing this important topic!

WHAT NUMEROLOGY IS

Stated simply, numerology *is the study of the energy of numbers, as revealed in the birth date and birth name of a person and their implications in that person's life.* When applied in business, it is referred to as Business Numerology, and reviews that same information (date of organization or incorporating and name of business) and explores the energy of the business as an entity. Your numerology profile is essentially your soul's agenda for this lifetime. And realizing what your numbers are – and how to get into sync with them in your life and work – is what leads to success.

The roots of numerology trace to the work of the mathematician and philosopher Pythagoras, born in 590 B.C. Primarily known for developing the Pythagorean Theorem – and in fact for inventing the entire field of geometry – he was a remarkable man in that he was the first to realize that the foundation of the universe is actually numbers. And he lived nearly 100 years, unheard of in that time! He posited that each number held a specific vibration, and that the vibration or tone at the moment each person is born has a significant impact on who they become and their life direction and choices. In addition, he introduced the now well-accepted principle that the numbers 1 through 9 represent key stages within the human life cycle, repeated throughout one's life.

The foundation built by Pythagoras was brought into the Western culture through a lineage of women. A devoted student of Pythagoras, Mrs. L. Dow Balliett, developed her own system of numbers in early 1900's based on the Pythagorean system. Mrs. Balliett is credited with westernizing the principles numerology. She in turn influenced Dr. Julia Seton, who brought the name "numerology" to the system. Dr. Seton is the mother of Dr. Juno Jordan, who led the California Institute of Numerical Research for 25 years and created a substantial body of research and additions to the system. Most modern numerology is based on the work of these women.

Numerology presupposes reincarnation, and that each soul is on its own path of evolution, choosing areas of mastery in each lifetime that will help it advance in its spiritual growth. However, you can gain remarkable insights about your life and work from numerology, even if you do not believe in reincarnation

THE RESURGENCE OF NUMEROLOGY TODAY

Numerology is 2500 years old – and yet interest in it along with other similar practices such as astrology, hand analysis, and tarot are enjoying a renaissance of interest, exploration and focus today. What is behind this resurgence?

Quest for meaning. Following the events of the "dot com bust" in 2000, the terrorist attacks on 9/11/01, and the recession of 2008-2011, many people's foundation was shaken – and life as they knew it was gone. Inevitably, times like this cause people to go within and seek a deeper meaning in life than what they can see, hear, taste and touch. So spiritual topics come to the forefront – especially with the "stacking" of several significant and life-changing events one after the other.

Rapid rise in conscious entrepreneurship. Entrepreneurship has been steadily increasing for more than three decades, with more than 500,000 businesses started every month, according to the Kauffman Foundation. In the past decade, an increasing trend is "conscious" or "purposeful" entrepreneurship, in which business owners seek to contribute to the greater good – and express and fulfill his/her life purpose – through their business. To do so requires that, as an entrepreneur or professional, you know what your purpose is, what kind of business or profession to start or grow, and how to align key events with your natural cycles. Numerology can help with this.

Feminine Model of Leadership in the corporate world. To a large extent, the old authoritarian "my way or the highway" leadership style has been overtaken by the Feminine Leadership Style. Female leaders have many of the same qualities as their male colleagues, especially an ability to set high goals and inspire others to fulfill them. But women are different in some particular ways that make them valuable additions to decision-making teams. For example, women are more motivated by the purpose or meaning of their work than men, who focus more on compensation and their job titles," according to Joanna Barsh, senior partner at McKinsey & Company and co-author of *How Remarkable Women Lead: A Breakthrough Model for Work and Life*. This has opened the door for disciplines such as numerology to be relied upon for product naming, launch planning, bank account number selection and more.

Intertwining of intuition and intellect in business. Beginning with Laura Day's Practical Intuition in the 1980's to the present day, intuition now has a role – along with the facts, analysis and hard data – in decision-making within both large corporations and entrepreneurial ventures. Just because something makes sense on paper doesn't mean it is the right choice if it doesn't feel right...or if the doors you want to open seem to be blocked when the company tries to move forward.

Rise of the coaching movement, with its focus on life purpose, as key to success and satisfaction. The origins of the life- and business-coaching industry began in 1989 when accountant Thomas Leonard began applying results-based coaching techniques with individuals. At that time, I was simultaneously pioneering the philosophy that life purpose is the key to fulfillment at work – whether that means working for someone else or for yourself. I founded Career Coach Institute in 2001 based on that philosophy - and at that time, it was a radical notion! Now, with more than 100,000 coaches worldwide and the International Coach Federation boasting more than 22,000 members, pursuing one's life purpose to create an extraordinary life has become commonplace. Numerology provides a window into your life purpose that eliminates the guesswork, and it nicely compliments coaching strategies.

Greater acceptance of spiritual concepts in the mainstream. Thanks to several emerging movements that are spiritual but not religious, spiritual concepts have moved into the mainstream. *Cultural Creatives*, published in 2001 by Paul Ray and Sherry Anderson, identified a group of individuals sharing key values such as ecological sustainability, concern about the condition of women and children, desire to rebuild neighborhoods and improve caring relationships, demand for authenticity and social conscience. It has grown from 23.6 percent of the US population in 1995 to nearly 35 percent, or 80 million people, now. Barbara Marx Hubbard's Shift Network, boasting more than 250,000 members, and other metaphysical churches and groups have fanned the movement toward spirituality as a key focus.

In short, the time is right, and the economic, psychological, spiritual and lifestyle moment is right for numerology to provide the insights millions of people like you are seeking to find meaning, wealth, and success in their lives.

HOW NUMEROLOGY CAN HELP YOU SUCCEED

Throughout this book, we will be exploring how you can use numerology to experience greater fulfillment, success and abundance. Here are some of the insights numerology can provide and how it will help you:Discover which of the 11 "Inspired Success Paths" is yours, and what types of business ventures and careers are ideal for you

- Know how and where to apply your talents so they will be most appreciated, feel best to you as you use them, and fulfill your Inspired life's purpose too

- Know when you are working the expressed side of your Inspired Success Path or the suppressed side of it, and how to get back on track

- Discover what the "ultimate outcome" of your life's work is – as written in your soul's agenda (so you can be sure you are heading toward satisfying it)

- Know how others perceive you when they first meet you so you can make the most of networking, marketing, sales and positioning opportunities

- Understand shifts in desired career, work and business direction in mid-life to make this transition easier

- Ensure that you fulfill any karma that is built into your profile so you don't have to repeat those lessons

- Learn how to dissolve the common energy blocks to your Inspired Success Path

- Learn how to transform beliefs that could sabotage or block your progress on your path

- Know what to name your business and its products, services or offerings so that it is in synch with your Inspired Success Path

- Understand the essential character of your business – and how others see it

- Time the incorporation date, launch dates, and other key events in alignment with the numerology profile of your business

- Identify your ideal tribe/market based on your numerology profile and that of your business

- Know what to do and what to delegate in your business based on your "planes of expression"

- Discover the ideal numerology profile of staff for various functions in your business, and be able to hire/contract based on that profile

- Understand the cycles of your own life and that of your business to align with optimum timing

Sound exciting? Let's get started!

2

DISCOVERING YOUR INSPIRED SUCCESS PATH™

If you have wondered what you were meant to do as your business or vocation, you have likely taken assessments, gone to seminars, read books, done journaling, hired consultants and more to find out. And if you are like many people with whom I work, you may be in midlife and still be confused about this key question in life...or find that you are ready for a shift or transition in your work or business, and are unsure about your direction.

Numerology can help you clarify your direction – and navigate key transitions in your work and life – by delving into the code hidden within your birth name and birth date. A key premise of numerology is that before you were born, your soul – the eternal part of you – created your life agenda. This *"Inspired Success Path"* includes *the primary talents you would bring into your life, the best avenues through which to express them, the key developmental stages and challenges you would face, and what your ultimate accomplishments would be.*

There are entire numerology-based career discovery systems based on just one of the six numbers in your core profile. And while this can provide some insights, the system you will learn here catalyzes two of these numbers to derive your Inspired Success Path, and in Part Three we explore the other four numbers and how they add spice and flavor to your core Path.

This approach aligns with the insights of Dr. Juno Jordan – the mother of modern numerology – about using numerology to determine one's vocation:

> "Some people have outstanding talents and are destined for a specialized line of work. On the other hand, most people seem to have many talents and can do many things, but fail to realize their true worth or capabilities. They go from one line of work to another until, by trial and error and many disappointments, they discover they do have talents, often too late in life. Many good and loyal workers could advance to a better position and gain their heart's desire if they would take time to 'know themselves.'

> "Vocational analysis is a matter of synchronization – to bring all the traits of character, the abilities, and the destiny into simultaneous alignment." – Dr. Juno Jordan, Numerology: The Romance in Your Name

There is a delightful synergy between the numbers that makes you who you are. And to look only at one number would be to attempt to reduce you to a single dimension, when in fact you live in three dimensions (and may be aware of more than that!).

CALCULATING YOUR INSPIRED SUCCESS PATH

To calculate your Inspired Success Path, you will need two pieces of information:

- Your full date of birth (month, day and year)
- Your full name at birth (including any middle names)

If you aren't a math whiz, don't worry! The two calculations you will do are simple – all you need to do is add single digits. And it's worth it to gain all of the insights it will give you!

YOUR LIFE PATH NUMBER

The first of the two numbers we will be combining is your *Life Path number – the natural talents and abilities that you brought to this lifetime.* These are things you can do without training – and which others may naturally rely on you to do because they know you are good at them.

To calculate your Life Path number, take the month, day and year and reduce each to a single digit; then combine them to reach a total.

Example: October 16, 1957

Month: October = month 10; to reduce to single digit add 1 + 0 = 1

Day: 16 = 1 + 6 = 7

Year: 1 + 9 + 5 + 7 = 22; 2 + 2 = 4

Result: 1 + 7 + 4 = 12; 1 + 2 = 3 Life Path

Exceptions:

- If the final number you get is an 11 or a 22, do not reduce it further – it is a master number (explained in chapters 12 and 13).

- If the final number you get is a 13, 14, 16 or 19, it is a karmic number, explained further in chapter 18. Express it as the number and its single digit sum with a / like this:

13/4

14/5

16/7

19/1

Go ahead and calculate your Life Path number now.

YOUR EXPRESSION NUMBER

The second number we will use in calculating your Inspired Success Path is your *Expression number – the area you sought to master, and through which you desire to express yourself, in this lifetime; the new experience.* This is your field of opportunity and what you must live up to in this lifetime. It too will bring to your life experiences, people and opportunities having to do with the energy of this number.

To calculate your Expression number, use these steps:

Using the chart below, assign a numeric value to each of the names in your birth name:

1	2	3	4	5	6	7	8	9
A	B	C	D	E	F	G	H	I
J	K	L	M	N	O	P	Q	R
S	T	U	V	W	X	Y	Z	

Example:

M A R J O R I E   A M Y   S M I T H

4 1 9 1 6 9 9 5   1 4 7   1 4 9 2 8

44 = 4 + 4 = 8   12 = 1 + 2 = 3   24 = 2 + 4 = 6

      8   3   6

8 + 3 + 6 = 17; 1 + 7 = 8 Expression

Exceptions:

- If the final number you get is an 11 or a 22, do not reduce it further – it is a master number (explained in chapters 12 and 13).

- If the final number you get is a 13, 14, 16 or 19, it is a karmic number, explained further in chapter 18. Express it as the number and its single digit sum with a / like this:

13/4

14/5

16/7

19/1

Go ahead and calculate your Expression number now.

HOW THE LIFE PATH AND EXPRESSION RELATE

Dr. Juno Jordan explains clearly how these two numbers synergize to form your Inspired Success Path:

> "The Lifepath and the Expression may be compared to a man going into business, but not yet established in trade. The Lifepath represents the stock on hand and the Expression is the business to be established. The numbers found in the Lifepath and Expression, even though very different in meaning and purpose, work together at all times and belong together." – Dr. Juno Jordan, Numerology: The Romance in Your Name (emphasis added)

Based on this fundamental principle of synchronization, we will consider your Life Path and Expression numbers together to comprise your Inspired Success Path.

YOUR INSPIRED SUCCESS PATH

To express your Life Path and Expression numbers as your Inspired Success Path, simply list them with a hyphen in between.

Examples:

1 life path and 5 expression = 1-5 Inspired Success Path

9 life path and 11 expression = 9-11 Inspired Success Path

Go ahead and calculate your Inspired Success Path now.

In the chapters which follow, we will explore each Path and its variations – i.e., each form of Expression – in depth.

FAMILIES OF INSPIRED SUCCESS PATHS

There are three groups of numbers within the Inspired Success Paths that are naturally compatible, since they share a common orientation. They are:

- Mentally-oriented Inspired Success Paths: 1, 5 and 7

- Creatively-oriented Inspired Success Paths: 3, 6 and 9

- Business-oriented Inspired Success Paths: 2, 4 and 8

So you may find people with whom you feel compatible by choosing those who are in the same orientation group or path.

(Note: a detailed personalized numerology reading and report is available through our web site: www.YourDivineGifts.com/numerology-readings)

SUCCESS BY THE NUMBERS

PART TWO:

THE 11 INSPIRED SUCCESS PATHS

In this Part, we will explore each of the Inspired Success Paths in detail, including:

- Traits of that Path – including variations
- What it looks like when expressed and when suppressed
- Types of jobs or businesses best suited to that path
- At least one example of that Inspired Success Path in real life

$$6 \quad 84$$
$$2\,1\,57$$
$$9\,\underset{0}{1}\,3\,7$$

3

INSPIRED SUCCESS PATH 1: THE CHARISMATIC THOUGHT LEADER

Marlene, an Inspired Success Path 1-8, grew up as the oldest of two daughters to an orthodontist. When her sister became mentally ill, Marlene pursued her path of independence in making new friends and handling the adjustments when her father moved the family across the country in mid-career. After getting her Certified Public Accountant credential and her MBA, she excelled at a Big Five accounting/consulting firm working with entrepreneurs, and was so inspired that she promised to become an entrepreneur herself one day. The "Midas touch" of her 8 Expression took her to work at major film and entertainment companies until she stopped to have a family. After her children were of an age that allowed her some time freedom, she took my Certified Career Coach training and is using her coaching skills to help entrepreneurs manage transition and the financial side of their business – right on track with her Path!

I too am an Inspired Success Path 1, born an oldest child, excelling at academics (but not at sports!), directing musical groups and later church boards and my own businesses. To help me hone the ability to stand on my own two feet, my parents called a family meeting when I was 12 and announced that we were moving to a new town and selling the farm I had grown up on because they had bought a business. This was traumatic for me – both because I had never lived anywhere else, and because I would have to make new friends and adjust to a new environment. Shortly after we moved, my dad was having horrendous headaches, and after returning home early from a square dance calling competition, he was diagnosed with brain cancer. Just 9 months later he died at the age of 37, leaving my mother to run the auto parts store in which she had planned to serve as bookkeeper – and leaving me to run the household!

That definitely forced me to grow up quickly, and to develop the inner strength that later served me well both as an executive and, for most of my career, as an entrepreneur and thought leader.

TRAITS OF THE INSPIRED SUCCESS PATH 1

Those with a 1 life path are born leaders. If you are a 1, you are motivated by a need for soul freedom and personal attainment. Your prime directive is to learn how to be independent from others in all ways, but especially emotionally and financially. Ones often have the potential to be great leaders, but often fail when it comes to teamwork and cooperation. For this reason, they make great entrepreneurs!

Independence comes naturally to the 1, and they will learn through their life experiences how to become a strong individual. This naturally leads to leadership opportunities. Ones should look for vocations that allow them to use their unique ideas and pioneer spirit. Status is important to the 1, and they possess a touch of the unusual. They need to avoid selfishness, conceit, and overzealous behavior. The best environment for a 1 is one where they are left "to their own devices." The 1 usually achieves much as long as their drive, creativity, and originality are well employed. They are best suited to leadership roles in their work.

Strong-willed and independent, 1's can be seen as bossy or overconfident if their inner strength is not tempered. They are focused on status and looking good, which can contribute to their drive to achieve.

(Note that if the 1 is a 10/1 or a 19/1 it could represent a Karmic Debt – see chapter 18.)

VARIATIONS ON THE INSPIRED SUCCESS PATH 1

1-1: A 1 Life Path with a 1 Expression has dual 1 energy, which intensifies both the positive and negative aspects of that energy. They will want to apply their leadership skills in an innovative way – perhaps pioneering a new industry, or segment thereof; starting their own business to meet an unmet need in the market; or leading a new technology firm that is blazing new ground. This requires courage, taking the initiative, being original, innovative, and taking charge. (Even if it feels scary at times!) A 1's talents include originality, creativity and the ability to launch plans into motion.

1-2: A 1 Life Path with a 2 Expression will want to apply their leadership skills in an industry and role that values collaboration, teamwork and harmony. They may actively mediate or negotiate – whether in politics, real estate or business - or they may comfort and soothe people in a counseling or customer service role. They will usually want to work with others, rather than alone, and to seek the balanced solution to any issues. They are the "power behind the throne."

1-3: A 1 Life Path with a 3 Expression will want to apply their leadership skills in an industry and role that involves creative arts, communication, or the media. These people are optimistic and upbeat and tell a story well. They need to be involved in working with others and communicating regularly via written or spoken word. They can be scattered, so need to learn to focus their interests in one main area.

1-4: A 1 Life Path with a 4 Expression will want to apply their leadership skills through an industry and role that requires or values organization and structure – perhaps one that is in a bit of chaos when this person arrives! They are drawn to such fields as accounting, finance, law, and operations management, as well as classical music and literature. They can see how things fit together better than any other type, but may need a nudge to think "outside of the box."

1-5: A 1 Life Path with a 5 Expression will want to apply their leadership skills through an industry and role that involves change, travel, and autonomy. They might be high-achieving traveling salespeople, travel agents, international relations experts, politicians, or even ministers. They are excellent communicators, and their biggest challenge is to avoid pursuing new experiences to such an extent that they lack focus when it is needed.

1-6: A 1 Life Path with a 6 Expression will want to apply their leadership skills through an industry and role that involves aesthetic beauty, a sense of family and connectedness, interior design, child care, animal care, or plants. 1-6's love people, and bring a nurturing presence with them wherever they go. They will naturally gravitate to a leadership skills role within the organizations, foundations or companies that address these areas.

1-7: A 1 Life Path with a 7 Expression will want to apply their leadership skills through an industry and role that gives them time and space to reflect, analyze and research. Heading up a think tank or scientific/medical research firm would be a great fit for 1-7. They love to delve deeply into a topic and learn all they can about it. 1-7's can also be drawn to metaphysical and spiritual roles and are often intuitive or psychic.

1-8: A 1 Life Path with an 8 Expression will want to apply their leadership skills through an industry and role that gives them authority and power, values financial gain, and allows them to activate their potential for greatness. They will be naturally successful in business and financial affairs, and are great planners. They may go through ups and downs to reach their desired success, but eventually they will get there, if they avoid seeking money for its own sake.

1-9: A 1 Life Path with a 9 Expression will want to apply their leadership skills through an industry and role that makes the world a better place. The 1-9 is a humanitarian and/or philanthropist, and leading a nonprofit – or charitable activities of a for-profit firm – is a great fit for them. They also often gravitate to leading theater, music, or artistic organizations.

1-11: A 1 Life Path with an 11 Expression will want to apply their leadership skills through an industry and role that connects the seen with the unseen, the conscious with the unconscious. They are Spiritual Messengers – since the 11 is a Master Number (see chapter 12) that often feel different from others, and need to find the place they fit in. They are natural teachers and may find themselves leading training, education or other teaching-related organizations.

1-22: A 1 Life Path with a 22 Expression will want to apply their leadership skills through an industry and role that offers a global shift and structure – or even builds something brand new. 1-22's have a huge vision for how to improve things, and as the Master Builder bringing the leadership skills energy of the 1 multiplies the potential impact the 1-22 can have on the world.

EXPRESSION AND SUPPRESSION OF THE INSPIRED SUCCESS PATH 1

Each Inspired Success Path can be either expressed or suppressed, depending on whether the person is working it positively or negatively. Following are the signs of both and what to do if your Path is the 1 and you have begun to suppress your gifts.

Inspired Success Path 1 Expressed

The expressive 1 steps into leadership and taking the initiative in their lives with ease. They are willing to take risks, exercise ambition, confidence, and charisma in their work as well as personal life. They do not mind being perceived as different, as they know this is part of innovation. They have a tremendous drive and seemingly endless energy. People want to follow 1's wherever they are going when they are expressing their creativity and initiative fully!

Inspired Success Path 1 Suppressed

When 1's feel blocked, they will shy away from leadership. And like a block in a pipe, the energy will build up until it demands release. It will either find its expression in the form of a new project or creative expression, or the 1 can find him/herself facing addiction. The other challenge for a 1 is insecurity, since being innovative demands feeling different from the crowd. This can express as aggressiveness or shyness, depending on the personality, to cover up the fear of rejection. And 1's don't like being told what to do!

To get unblocked, the questions to ask are, "What do I want to start now?" or "Where do I need to step up and lead now?"

JOBS OR BUSINESSES BEST SUITED TO THE INSPIRED SUCCESS PATH 1

Knowing that the 1, the Charismatic Thought Leader, must be in a leadership role, following are some of the roles they are well suited for:

- Entrepreneur (any type) because it lets them carve their own course

- CEO (any industry – modified by the Expression number as listed above)

- Other C-level or leadership positions

- Innovative industries where they can express their creative initiative and be rewarded for it

- Physician

- Executive Director of charitable organization

- Inventor

- Professional Speaker

SUCCESS BY THE NUMBERS

6 8 4
2 1 5 7
9 0 3 3

4

INSPIRED SUCCESS PATH 2: THE PEACEFUL MEDIATOR/ HARMONIZER

Helena, an Inspired Success Path 2-11, was a doctor who helped patients in a general practice – a natural role for someone on this Path. Just before coming to me, she had sold the medical practice where she unsuccessfully tried to bring a holistic perspective to her conservative specialty. Her intention was to help medical practitioners in her country think outside the traditional box of silo thinking and consider the whole person in their practice – but her idea was ahead of its time.

As we worked together further, I learned that she had successfully overcome cancer in recent years, and in the process had developed specialized knowledge in mind/body healing. Helena's passion began to redirect itself to helping cancer survivors reestablish harmony within themselves, reconnect to their passions and purpose, and create a new cancer-free lifestyle after their treatment was complete. She saw cancer as a gateway to spiritual realizations and awareness –

which perfectly depict the 2 Path with a Master 11/2 Expression, the Spiritual Messenger. She knew she had a big, important message to share with her clients about the personal growth opportunity their cancer could be – and we set about creating her business to do just that.

TRAITS OF THE INSPIRED SUCCESS PATH 2

The 2 Life Path naturally brings peace, harmony and cooperation to every situation. Initially they will learn lessons around cooperation, compromise and peacekeeping, and then will move on to drawing others together. Twos are extremely sensitive, perceptive, and somewhat shy. They can feel other people's feelings and be very empathetic (which, if they don't set healthy boundaries, can lead to codependence and self-depletion).

Twos have an inherent sense of morality and fairness, they tend to be indecisive as they can clearly see both sides of any conundrum or argument. These loving, optimistic individuals prefer to see only the best in others. They are honest almost to a fault. They have highly developed emotional sensitivity and thrive best in a work setting that requires teamwork.

Their soul's agenda is to create harmony and peace, find balance, seek cooperation and be a team player. Lessons around relationship will abound with a 2 Expression, such as how to be gentle and emotionally receptive. Twos act with tact and insight into both personalities and situations, and have a highly developed intuition. Twos can be thrown off balance by a single unkind word, due to their sensitivity. Twos prefer to be the person behind the scenes versus in a public role.

Diplomacy and sensitivity characterize the Two, and they can be quite persuasive! As entrepreneurs, they are great at mediation, coaching, teaching, or any role where they bring people into harmony. They are natural collectors too! And they can be perfectionists when it comes to home and work environment.

VARIATIONS ON THE INSPIRED SUCCESS PATH 2

2-1: A 2 Life Path with a 1 Expression will want to apply their peacemaking abilities in a leadership capacity – perhaps bringing harmony to a splintered company or industry. They may be drawn to a leadership role in entrepreneurial venture in a peacemaking field such as counseling, coaching, or mediation. They can bring innovation to any venture they are involved with – or any client with whom they work. But they must take the initiative to create something new, to exercise leadership and independence to feel fulfilled. The 1 Expression brings such talents as originality, creativity and the ability to launch plans into motion to the 2's innate talents.

2-2: A 2 Life Path with a 2 Expression has the double energy of the Two, which intensifies both the positive and negative aspects of that energy. They will want to apply their peacemaking abilities in an industry and role that values collaboration, teamwork and harmony. They may actively mediate or negotiate – whether in politics, real estate or business - or they may comfort and soothe people in a counseling or customer service role. They will usually want to work with others, rather than alone, and to seek the balanced solution to any issues. Being part of a strong partnership (whether personal or professional) is important to them.

2-3: A 2 Life Path with a 3 Expression will want to apply their peacemaking abilities in an industry and role that involves creative arts, communication, or the media. These people are optimistic and upbeat, and they tell a story well. They are well-liked, look younger than their age, and can reawaken others' passion in life. 2-3's can be scattered, so need to learn to focus their interests in one main area.

2-4: A 2 Life Path with a 4 Expression will want to apply their peacemaking abilities through an industry and role that requires or values organization and structure. They can easily see how ideas can become reality, and are excellent at planning and implementation. They are drawn to such fields as accounting, finance, law, and operations management, as well as classical music and literature. They may need a nudge to think "outside of the box" so they do not become too rule-bound.

2-5: A 2 Life Path with a 5 Expression will want to apply their peacemaking abilities through an industry and role that involves change, travel, and autonomy. They might be involved in sales, public relations, travel or entertainment – the more new experiences the better! And being enthusiastic about what a new experience (whether a trip or a software program) can bring a prospective customer comes naturally to the 2-5! They are excellent communicators, and their biggest challenge is to avoid pursuing new experiences to such an extent that they lack focus when it is needed.

2-6: A 2 Life Path with a 6 Expression will want to apply their peacemaking abilities through an industry and role that involves aesthetic beauty, a sense of family and connectedness, interior design, child care, animal care, or plants. 2-6's love people, and bring a nurturing presence with them wherever they go. They can have a humanitarian outlook, and will naturally gravitate to a peacemaking role within the organizations, foundations or companies that address these areas.

2-7: A 2 Life Path with a 7 Expression will want to apply their peacemaking abilities through an industry and role focusing on education, teaching, or a spiritual entity. They need them time and space to reflect, analyze and research. Heading up a think tank or scientific/medical research firm would be a great fit for 2-7. They seek to find the answers to life's questions, and love to delve deeply into a topic and learn all they can about it. 2-7's can also be drawn to metaphysical and spiritual roles and are often intuitive or psychic.

2-8: A 2 Life Path with an 8 Expression will want to apply their peacemaking abilities through an industry and role that gives them authority and power, values financial gain, and allows them to activate their potential for greatness. They could feel some conflict between their natural tendency to be the power behind the throne, and the 8's desire to be on the throne. 2-8's are naturally successful in business and financial affairs, and are great planners. They do things for the love of doing them, rather than strictly for the money. They may go through ups and downs to reach their desired success, and must be careful not to seek money or power for their own sake.

2-9: A 2 Life Path with a 9 Expression will want to apply their peacemaking abilities through an industry and role that makes the world a better place. The 2-9 is a humanitarian and/or philanthropist, and contributing within a nonprofit – or charitable activities of a for-profit firm – is a great fit for them. They also often gravitate to working within theater, music, or artistic organizations. Their key lesson is learning to apply their talents for the good of the whole, rather than for personal gain.

2-11: A 2 Life Path with an 11 Expression will want to apply their peacemaking abilities through an industry and role that connects the seen with the unseen, the conscious with the unconscious. They are very emotionally aware, and are in fact spiritual illuminators that often feel different from others, and need to find the place they fit in. They are natural teachers and may find themselves leading training, education or other teaching-related organizations.

2-22: A 2 Life Path with a 22 Expression will want to apply their peacemaking abilities through an industry and role that offers a global shift and structure – or even builds something brand new. 2-22's have a huge vision for how to create harmony on a grand scale – it is as though the 2 energy was tripled in its intensity with this combination. And this Master Builder energy intensifies and multiplies the potential impact the 2-22 can have on the world.

EXPRESSION AND SUPPRESSION OF THE INSPIRED SUCCESS PATH 2

Each Inspired Success Path can be either expressed or suppressed, depending on whether the person is working it positively or negatively. Following are the signs of both and what to do if your Path is the Two and you have begun to suppress your gifts.

Inspired Success Path 2 Expressed

The expressive Two is a delight to be around, since they are someone who understands others' feelings and needs and are great listeners. When people have problems, they will come to 2's for the answer. (So a great career or business field is one that allows them to do this for a living!) They are closely connected to both a life partner and a partner in business – either formally as co-owners of a business or as a "right-hand person" to an executive, leader or business owner. They beautify their surroundings – whether office or home. They help people with different points of view come to a compromise and learn to cooperate instead of compete. They are loyal, dependable, and service-oriented.

Inspired Success Path 2 Suppressed

When 2's suppress their natural flow, they can become blaming or codependent, depending on the other dimensions of their personality and the person involved. After giving tirelessly of themselves for months or years, they cry "uncle!" when they begin to feel too depleted to give any more. They are susceptible to the demands of others to the exclusion of their own needs, and struggle to set healthy boundaries that allow their sense of self to remain intact. They may even define themselves by the supportive role they play with others.

The best remedy for 2's facing these issues is to get honest about what they really wants – apart from what others' expectations or perceptions might be – and act in their own behalf.

To get unblocked, the questions to ask are: "What do I really want and need?" and "What needs to be harmonized now?"

JOBS OR BUSINESSES BEST SUITED TO THE INSPIRED SUCCESS PATH 2

Knowing that the 2, the Peaceful Mediator/Harmonizer, must be in a peacemaking role, following are some of the roles they are well suited for:

- Judge

- Mediator

- Lawyer

- Coaching or counseling

- Social work

- Ministry

- Diplomat

- Interior design or other fields involving beautification of the environment

6 8 4
2 1 5 7
9 1 3 7
o 3

5

INSPIRED SUCCESS PATH 3: THE CREATIVE COMMUNICATOR

John, an Inspired Success Path 3-11, was born to a middle class family in southern California. He learned early that he excelled at conversation, persuasion, storytelling and sports – but not at academics. So he used his charm and conversational abilities – as well as his outstanding performance at football and other sports – to get into the "in" crowd at school. His initial foray at college was unsuccessful, since he was more interested in dating than studying. But after starting his family and getting clearer on his desired career – having dabbled in several jobs by the time he was 30 – he returned to college and got his industrial engineering degree.

As he pursued his career, he served as a project manager for a large health care organization, using his relationship-building to keep contractors happy and projects on time and on schedule. He was later hired by one of the emerging tech giants in their infancy and managed large projects for them - involving multiple contractors as well as internal customers to coordinate - until he retired.

TRAITS OF THE INSPIRED SUCCESS PATH 3

John is a quintessential 3 Life Path in that he used his people skills to succeed in an environment that focused largely on productivity, numbers and results. The 3 brings creativity and communication as its natural talents. (So many writers, poets, actors and musicians have this life path.) Often the "life of the party," the 3 sometimes squanders its talent in being a social butterfly. Initially they will master optimism and enthusiasm, as well as appropriate emotional expression. They will then begin to inspire others with their gifts. Example: they will help people see the joy in any situation.

Storytelling comes naturally to the 3, and they bring a creative flair to every task. Public acknowledgement of their unique talent makes their path complete. Number 3's are also excellent chefs and hosts and boast exquisite taste in fashion and home decoration. They are often sought after socially.

Usually a number 3 is quite stubborn and plays to win no matter how high the cost of success. Their unusual stamina and vigor makes it easier for them to rebound from setbacks in life than most people. Often these setbacks are of a financial or romantic nature as their idealism and spontaneity sometimes causes them to make bad choices.

VARIATIONS ON THE INSPIRED SUCCESS PATH 3

3-1: A 3 Life Path with a 1 Expression will want to apply their creativity and communication talents by taking leadership or designing innovative solutions – perhaps pioneering a new industry, starting their own business, or otherwise taking a role in which they manage others or lead an initiative. This requires courage, being willing to start something new, being original, innovative, and taking charge. The 1 Expression adds originality, creativity and the ability to launch plans into motion.

3-2: A 3 Life Path with a 2 Expression will want to apply their creativity and communication in an industry and role that values collaboration, teamwork and harmony. They may actively mediate or negotiate – whether in politics, real estate or business - or they may comfort and soothe people in a counseling or customer service role. They will usually want to work with others, rather than alone; to seek the balanced solution to any issues; and to be "behind the scenes" unlike the 3-1 that wants to be out in front.

3-3: A 3 Life Path with a 3 Expression has dual 3 energy, which intensifies both the positive and negative aspects of that energy. They will want to apply their creativity and communication in a classic creative and communication industries such as the media, entertainment, public relations and the like. They may have lessons to learn so they can effectively express their emotions through their natural gift of words. Threes often find themselves being writers, speakers, musicians or actors to utilize their natural talent for self-expression. Their challenge is not to scatter their talents – concentration and focus are key to their success.

3-4: A 3 Life Path with a 4 Expression will want to apply their creativity and communication through an industry and role that requires or values organization and structure. This can create a conflict, since the 3 Life Path calls for coloring outside the lines and expressing creativity, when the 4 Expression seeks rules, order, and structure. 3-4's are drawn to such fields as accounting, finance, law, and operations management, as well as classical music and literature. They can see how things fit together using their 4 Expression, and can apply this in artistic or business pursuits to design functional yet innovative products and services.

3-5: A 3 Life Path with a 5 Expression will want to apply their creativity and communication through an industry and role that involves change, travel, and autonomy. They might be traveling salespeople, travel agents, international relations experts, politicians, or eve ministers. They are excellent communicators, and their biggest challenge is to avoid pursuing new experiences to such an extent that they lack focus when it is needed.

3-6: A 3 Life Path with a 6 Expression will want to apply their creativity and communication through an industry and role that involves aesthetic beauty, a sense of family and connectedness, interior design, child care, animal care, or plants. 3-6's love people, and bring a nurturing presence with them wherever they go. They will naturally gravitate to a creativity and communication role within the organizations, foundations or companies that address these areas.

3-7: A 3 Life Path with a 7 Expression will want to apply their creativity and communication through an industry and role that gives them time and space to reflect, analyze and research. Working in an educational or research firm would be a great fit for 3-7. They love to delve deeply into a topic and learn all they can about it. 3-7's can also be drawn to metaphysical and spiritual roles and are often intuitive or psychic.

3-8: A 3 Life Path with an 8 Expression will want to apply their creativity and communication through an industry and role that gives them authority and power, values financial gain, and allows them to activate their potential for greatness. 3-8's are naturally successful in business and financial affairs, and are great planners. They do things for the love of doing them, rather than strictly for the money. They may go through ups and downs to reach their desired success, and must be careful not to seek money or power for their own sake.

3-9: A 3 Life Path with a 9 Expression will want to apply their creativity and communication through an industry and role that makes the world a better place. The 3-9 is a humanitarian and/or philanthropist, and contributing within a nonprofit – or charitable activities of a for-profit firm – is a great fit for them. They also often gravitate to working within theater, music, or artistic organizations. Their key lesson is learning to apply their talents for the good of the whole, rather than for personal gain.

3-11: A 3 Life Path with an 11 Expression will want to apply their creativity and communication through an industry and role that connects the seen with the unseen, the conscious with the unconscious. They are very emotionally aware, and in fact bring spiritual illumination. As a result,

they often feel different from others, and need to find the place they fit in. They are natural teachers and may find themselves leading training, education or other teaching-related organizations.

3-22: A 3 Life Path with a 22 Expression will want to apply their creativity and communication through an industry and role that offers a global shift and structure — or even builds something brand new. 3-22's have a huge vision for how to improve things, and as the Master Builder bringing the creativity and communication energy of the 1 multiplies the potential impact the 3-22 can have on the world.

EXPRESSION AND SUPPRESSION OF THE INSPIRED SUCCESS PATH 3

Each Inspired Success Path can be either expressed or suppressed, depending on whether the person is working it positively or negatively. Following are the signs of both and what to do if your Path is the 3 and you have begun to suppress your gifts.

Inspired Success Path 3 Expressed

Expressive 3's share their creativity freely and enthusiastically - and are handsomely rewarded in doing so. They are surrounded by loving friends and are sought after for social gatherings. Looking younger than their age, they thrive in social settings. They trust their intuitive instincts and ideas and can rally others to support their large visions, using their powers of persuasion. Their communication abilities serve them not only to share information, but to convey emotions — and help others connect with their own emotional realities.

Inspired Success Path 3 Suppressed

When 3's feel blocked, they may withdraw into a private space of silence to nurse hurt feelings. Alternately, they may become critical of others when they are in fact covering up their own insecurities. Shying away from public speaking or crowds can be other earmarks of a blocked 3 Path. Due to their emotional sensitivity, 3's need to learn to shield themselves from taking on others' energy – and until they do, they may feel drained or depleted and not know why. 3's are unduly susceptible to criticism, as well as self-doubt. An emotional roller coaster can characterize the suppressed 3 until they learn to confidently communicate their reality, avoid taking on others' energy and exercise their creative expertise.

To get unblocked, the questions to ask are, "What do I want to create now?" or "What do I need to communicate now?"

JOBS OR BUSINESSES BEST SUITED TO THE INSPIRED SUCCESS PATH 3

Knowing that the 3, the Creative Communicator, must be in a creative role, following are some of the roles they are well suited for:

- Public relations
- Sales
- Advertising
- Acting
- Writing
- Artist
- Publishing

- Counseling or coaching
- Entertainment
- Speaking
- Teaching
- Chef

SUCCESS BY THE NUMBERS

$$\begin{matrix} & 6 & 8 & 4 \\ 2 & & 5 & 7 \\ 9 & 1 & & \\ & & 3 & \end{matrix}$$

6

INSPIRED SUCCESS PATH 4:
THE HARD-WORKING
SYSTEMS THINKER/BUILDER

Lonnie, an Inspired Success Path 4-1, came to me at a crossroads in her career. As a teenager, she had the normal confusion about what her career path would be. Then one day she visited a pathology museum at the university and saw the containers that housed the babies with congenital abnormalities – and in a flash of insight she knew she was destined to study medicine. She set her course and became a licensed ob/gyn doctor. All the while, she struggled with depression and was treated with antidepressant medication (which from a numerological standpoint could indicate her reluctance to step into her 1 Expression as a leader in her field).

Years into her practice, in her 4 personal year (see chapter 24 for details, but know that this timing intensifies the 4 life path energy), she had another turning point experience. She had felt that her job was the right overall focus, but something within her was not being expressed in her daily activities. While traveling in a remote part of

India, she encountered a tourist who had collapsed with what was later diagnosed as an aortic aneurysm. Lonnie kept her alive for 48 hours using guidance from her intuition until she was airlifted by helicopter. She suddenly realized that what was missing in her practice was a spiritual connection, and when she met me (at age 44 – note the intensified 4 energy again) she was preparing to open a spiritual counseling and training business for pregnant mothers to help them connect directly with the soul of their baby in utero. And this will no doubt establish new precedents and innovative services (called for by the 1 Expression) as it emerges.

TRAITS OF THE INSPIRED SUCCESS PATH 4

The 4 Life Path brings natural skills in organization, developing systems, building a foundation, and working hard. (And what better field to apply that than in medicine as Lonnie did?) Practical and down to earth, 4's have strong ideas about right and wrong. Initially mastering the benefits of following the rules and being loyal, they then move on to building systems for the long term. Fours want "i's dotted and t's crossed" and can be compulsive about details. Others look to the 4 for help in organizing things and managing projects.

Values such as justice, honesty, tenacity, and perseverance are key to the 4. Fours can be rigid in their ideas, sometimes too quick to judge – but are loyal to those they love. They develop long-term relationships and handle money well. They must be careful not to be bossy, however – or to work so hard that they don't get to enjoy life. Their career success often comes in banking, accounting, management, and similar fields.

They desire to build something of lasting value. Fours learn to be practical, to work hard, and to establish and maintain order and convention while doing so. They express stability, steadfastness, and dependability. They are great at managing and organizing, whether it is a business, a family, a project or a political campaign. Fours are systematic and methodical in their approach to business, life, and problems. They use their highly developed sense of structure to turn dreams into reality. Their weakness can be getting too focused on the details and losing sight of the bigger picture. They can also be overworkers or workaholics.

VARIATIONS ON THE INSPIRED SUCCESS PATH 4

4-1: A 4 Life Path with a 1 Expression will want to apply their systems thinking skills using leadership in some way – either leading an organization that has systems in place and needs a capable leader, or a company in chaos needing structure, systems and order restored. This requires courage, taking the initiative, being original, innovative, and taking charge. The 1 Expression adds originality, creativity and the ability to launch plans into motion.

4-2: A 4 Life Path with a 2 Expression will want to apply their systems thinking skills in an industry and role that values collaboration, teamwork and harmony. They may actively mediate or negotiate – whether in politics, real estate or business - or they may comfort and soothe people in a counseling or customer service role. They will usually want to work with others, rather than alone, and to seek the balanced solution to any issues.

4-3: A 4 Life Path with a 3 Expression will want to apply their systems thinking skills in an industry and role that involves creative arts, communication, or the media. 4-3's are optimistic and upbeat, with exceptional communication skills. They can be very creative, and seek to either bring a solid foundation to an unstructured arts or creative firm, or to rally support for new systems through using their powers of persuasion. They can be scattered, so need to learn to focus their interests in one main area.

4-4: A 4 Life Path with a 4 Expression has the double 4 energy, which intensifies both the positive and negative aspects of that energy. They can tend to be more compulsive and rule-bound than other 4's, so will want to beware of "black and white" thinking. They are drawn to such fields as accounting, finance, law, and operations management, as well as classical music and literature. They can see how things fit together better than any other type, but may need a nudge to bend the rules or think creatively.

4-5: A 4 Life Path with a 5 Expression will want to apply their systems thinking skills through an industry and role that involves change, travel, and autonomy. They will attract lessons and experiences requiring that they adapt to fast-changing circumstances. Learning to think on their feet and be resourceful is a must! They love to seek new experiences and live fully, and their biggest challenge is to avoid pursuing the next new thing to such an extent that they lack focus when it is needed.

4-6: A 4 Life Path with a 6 Expression will want to apply their systems thinking skills through an industry and role that involves aesthetic beauty, a sense of family and connectedness, interior design, child care, animal care, or plants. 4-6's love people, and bring a nurturing presence with them wherever they go. They will naturally gravitate to a systems thinking skills role within the organizations, foundations or companies that address these areas.

4-7: A 4 Life Path with a 7 Expression will want to apply their systems thinking skills through an industry and role that gives them time and space to reflect, analyze and research. Working in a university, think tank or scientific/medical research firm would be a great fit for 4-7. They love to delve deeply into a topic and learn all they can about it. 4-7's can also be drawn to metaphysical and spiritual roles and are often intuitive or psychic.

4-8: A 4 Life Path with an 8 Expression will want to apply their systems thinking skills through an industry and role that gives them authority and power, values financial gain, and allows them to activate their potential for greatness. They will be naturally successful in business and financial affairs, and are great planners. They may go through ups and downs to reach their desired success, but eventually they will get there, if they avoid seeking money for its own sake.

4-9: A 4 Life Path with a 9 Expression will want to apply their systems thinking skills through an industry and role that makes the world a better place. The 4-9 is a humanitarian and/or philanthropist, and leading a nonprofit – or charitable activities of a for-profit firm – is a great fit for them. They also often gravitate to positions in theater, music, or artistic organizations.

4-11: A 4 Life Path with an 11 Expression will want to apply their systems thinking skills through an industry and role that connects the seen with the unseen, the conscious with the unconscious. They are spiritual illuminators that often feel different from others, and need to find the place they fit in. They are natural teachers and may find themselves leading training, education or other teaching-related organizations.

4-22: A 4 Life Path with a 22 Expression will want to apply their systems thinking skills through an industry and role that offers a global shift and structure – or even builds something brand new. 4-22's have a huge vision for how to improve things, and as the Master Builder bringing the systems thinking skills energy of the 1 multiplies the potential impact the 4-22 can have on the world.

EXPRESSION AND SUPPRESSION OF THE INSPIRED SUCCESS PATH 4

Each Inspired Success Path can be either expressed or suppressed, depending on whether the person is working it positively or negatively. Following are the signs of both and what to do if your Path is the 4 and you have begun to suppress your gifts.

Inspired Success Path 4 Expressed

Expressive 4's have a plan and is implementing it. They are about the business of building something lasting that is important to them and helps others. They are infinitely patient and willing to put in the hard work and sustained effort to reach the desired goal, overcoming the obstacles along the way. Each project resembles a construction project, and the 4 can both design the blueprint and oversee the stages of the building to a successful completion.

Inspired Success Path 4 Suppressed

When 4's feel blocked, they may become rigid in their thinking and not open to alternatives that would save time, money or energy – or all three. They can also find themselves obsessively focusing on one small aspect of a project or system, unwilling to broaden their view to the larger perspective. When they feel frustrated by the amount of work it takes to complete an assignment or project, they may be tempted to skip steps or find a shortcut, but somehow feel they are "cheating" by not doing everything in a linear, step-by-step fashion. "Anal-retentive" or OCD are terms that describe the stuck 4.

To get unblocked, the questions to ask are, "What do I want to build now?" or "What do I need to organize now?"

JOBS OR BUSINESSES BEST SUITED TO THE INSPIRED SUCCESS PATH 4

Knowing that the 4, the Hard-Working Systems Thinker/Builder, must be in a systems design and implementation role, following are some of the roles they are well suited for:

- Engineer
- Lawyer

- Physician

- Operations manager

- Project manager

- Facilities manager

- Manufacturing – especially quality control and process design

- Real estate, architecture or construction

- Finance

- Software programmer

- Mechanical fields

$$2\,{}^{6}_{9}\!{}^{8\,4}_{1}\,{}^{5}_{0}\!{}^{7}_{3}$$

7

INSPIRED SUCCESS PATH 5: THE VISIONARY CHANGE AGENT

Sam, an Inspired Success Path 5-1, grew up in a rural area of the Midwestern U.S. His family struggled financially, but always had enough to get by. As soon as he graduated high school, he moved to Los Angeles, California and got into sales. He worked for a national company with multiple branches, selling financial services to businesses. Sam excelled at the job, since every day was different - he never knew when he woke up where he would be, who he would talk to, or what exciting things the day would hold.

He rapidly progressed and became salesperson of the month for the Los Angeles branch, and when the opportunity arose to move to Hawaii – and be sales manager there – he jumped at the chance. He continued to expand his reach within the company and became a well-respected Vice President of the company at a record young age.

TRAITS OF THE INSPIRED SUCCESS PATH 5

Sam's career demonstrates the 5 Life Path at its best: autonomy and freedom in his career of sales, travel and new experiences on a regular basis. His 1 Expression also came into view as he excelled in his initial sales career and later management. Those on the 5 Path embrace change and seek freedom. They love travel, adventure, meeting new people, and adapting to changing circumstances. They indeed move into championing freedom for others as their life progresses. They are forward thinking, liberal, and resourceful – and may be good at many different professions.

Their career should have them working with the public in some way (advertising, publicity, sales, marketing etc.). Fives have a way with words and an inborn ability to motivate others. They lack discipline, however, and often struggle with addiction or impulsiveness. Discipline and focus are keys to their success so that they can follow through on that which they begin. Their challenge is to learn the true meaning of freedom – with balance. They learn from their direct experiences as the primary teacher.

(Note that if your 5 is a 14/5 it is a Karmic number, discussed in chapter 18.)

The 5's soul agenda is to change, adapt and progress. They welcome freedom – even seek it out – and travel, and follow their curiosity where it leads. However, they may struggle to find the balance between healthy discipline and loose boundaries. They are quite resourceful and are described as a "free spirit." If they use freedom properly, 5's can not only have diverse and fun life experiences, but enjoyable work too. However, the amount of change in their lives can seem overwhelming at times and they sometimes turn to addiction to cope. They need to learn to finish what they start. Fives are multitalented, with skills in many areas.

VARIATIONS ON THE INSPIRED SUCCESS PATH 5

5-1: A 5 Life Path with a 1 Expression will want to apply their adaptability and change management talents through leadership, as in the example of Sam above. They will be given lessons and experiences to help them both adapt to sudden change and to learn to stand on their own two feet. They may have difficulty putting down roots, but eventually need to focus their efforts to avoid being a "jack of all trades but master of none." The 1 Expression adds talents in include originality, creativity and the ability to launch plans into motion.

5-2: A 5 Life Path with a 2 Expression will want to apply their adaptability and change management talents in an industry and role that values collaboration, teamwork and harmony. They may actively mediate or negotiate – whether in politics, real estate or business - or they may comfort and soothe people in a counseling or customer service role. They will usually want to work with others, rather than alone, and to seek the balanced solution to any issues.

5-3: A 5 Life Path with a 3 Expression will want to apply their adaptability and change management talents in an industry and role that involves creative arts, communication, or the media. These people are optimistic and upbeat and tell a story well. They can be scattered, so need to learn to focus their interests in one main area.

5-4: A 5 Life Path with a 4 Expression will want to apply their adaptability and change management talents through an industry and role that requires or values organization and structure – perhaps where there has just been a merger or acquisition and they are attempting to combine cultures and systems. They are drawn to such fields as accounting, finance, law, and operations management, as well as classical music and literature. They can see how things fit together, and want to make lasting change through the systems they build.

5-5: A 5 Life Path with a 5 Expression has the dual 5 energy, which intensifies both the positive and negative aspects of that energy. They will want to apply their adaptability and change management talents through an industry and role that involves change, travel, and autonomy. They might be salespeople, travel agents, international relations experts, politicians, or eve ministers. They are excellent communicators, and their biggest challenge is to avoid pursuing new experiences to such an extent that they lack focus when it is needed.

5-6: A 5 Life Path with a 6 Expression will want to apply their adaptability and change management talents through an industry and role that involves aesthetic beauty, a sense of family and connectedness, interior design, child care, animal care, or plants. 5-6's love people, and bring a nurturing presence with them wherever they go. They will naturally gravitate to roles within the organizations, foundations or companies that provide care of others, beauty or community.

5-7: A 5 Life Path with a 7 Expression will want to apply their adaptability and change management talents through an industry and role that gives them time and space to reflect, analyze and research. Working in a scientific or medical research firm or in a progressive IT industry that is developing new technology would be a great fit for 1-7. They love to delve deeply into a topic and learn all they can about it. 5-7's can also be drawn to metaphysical and spiritual roles and are often intuitive or psychic.

5-8: A 5 Life Path with an 8 Expression will want to apply their adaptability and change management talents through an industry and role that gives them authority and power, values financial gain, and allows them to activate their potential for greatness. They will be naturally successful in business and financial affairs, and are great planners. They may go through ups and downs to reach their desired success, but eventually they will get there, if they avoid seeking money for its own sake.

5-9: A 5 Life Path with a 9 Expression will want to apply their adaptability and change management talents through an industry and role that makes the world a better place. The 5-9 is a humanitarian and/or philanthropist, and a role within a nonprofit whose role it is to make global change – or charitable activities of a for-profit firm – is a great fit for them. They also often gravitate to theater, music, or artistic organizations.

5-11: A 5 Life Path with an 11 Expression will want to apply their adaptability and change management talents through an industry and role that connects the seen with the unseen, the conscious with the unconscious. They are spiritual illuminators that often feel different from others, and need to find the place they fit in. They are natural teachers and may find themselves in training, education or other teaching-related organizations.

5-22: A 5 Life Path with a 22 Expression will want to apply their adaptability and change management talents through an industry and role that offers a global shift and structure – or even builds something brand new. 5-22's have a huge vision for how to improve things, and as the Master Builder bringing the adaptability and change management talents energy of the 5 multiplies the potential impact the 5-22 can have in global transformation.

EXPRESSION AND SUPPRESSION OF THE INSPIRED SUCCESS PATH 5

Each Inspired Success Path can be either expressed or suppressed, depending on whether the person is working it positively or negatively. Following are the signs of both and what to do if your Path is the 5 and you have begun to suppress your gifts.

Inspired Success Path 5 Expressed

Expressive 5's manage change like a yachtsman navigates a churning river. They adapt, change course when needed, and set the boundaries that are best for their own growth and expression. They seek out – and fully enjoy – new experiences in life, whether it is bungee jumping, an African safari, or meeting a new person. They exercise a healthy self-discipline while incorporating variety into their daily routine. They see life as a glorious adventure, here to be tasted, felt and experienced. They realize as much inner freedom as they allow themselves in their outer lives.

Inspired Success Path 5 Suppressed

When 5's feel blocked, they often pursue new experiences and feelings to excess – and may become prone to addictions. "If a little is good, more is better," is their motto. This leads them to find the balance of healthy boundaries they need to discover if they are to reach equilibrium in life. 5's may also draw someone into their life that restricts their full expression, whether parent, spouse or boss. This is the other end of the spectrum in finding balance between work and play, limits and no limits. They may find themselves pursuing so many different things at once that no one activity or business focus gets their best energy – which will frustrate them in time.

To get unblocked, the best questions to ask are, "What do I want to change or experience now?" or "What do I need to adapt to now to grow?"

JOBS OR BUSINESSES BEST SUITED TO THE INSPIRED SUCCESS PATH 5

Knowing that the 5, the Visionary Change Agent, must be in an ever-changing, evolving role. Following are some of the industries and positions they are well suited for:

- Sales careers
- Customer service
- Speaking
- Real estate
- Marketing
- Politics
- Public Relations
- Ministry
- Entertainment law
- Ecommerce sales and service
- Journalist

SUCCESS BY THE NUMBERS

$$6^84$$
$$2\,1^{5}7$$
$$9\,1_{0}3_{3}$$

8

INSPIRED SUCCESS PATH 6: THE NURTURING COMMUNITY BUILDER

Julie, an Inspired Success Path 6-1, was born the last of three children to her parents before they divorced. When her mother remarried, she had another daughter 10 years later but, as a working mother, Julie found herself babysitting her younger half-sister much of the time during her teenage years. This honed Julie's nurturing abilities at a relatively early age – in addition to the stray cats she always seemed to be taking in and adopting!

When Julie married, she had a son, David, who sailed through grammar school and junior high, but when he reached high school age he found himself at a personal crisis. He started using drugs, his behavior changed, and he virtually stopped doing his school work. Julie and her husband Mark got counseling help for David as well as for the entire family. As she learned to identify and master her own codependent behaviors, Julie was able to give her son the additional nurturing he needed and he successfully entered college and went on to start a career that was well aligned with his skills.

Other parents started reaching out to her with questions when they found out what had happened with David. Julie decided to go to coaching school and begin working with other parents dealing with teens who had lost their way – whether through substance abuse or other paths. She used her leadership skills (the 1 Expression number) to pioneer a new approach to teen coaching that became known worldwide.

TRAITS OF THE INSPIRED SUCCESS PATH 6

Julie depicts the 6 Life Path in that nurturing – of people and animals – has been a theme throughout her life. They focus on "home and hearth," and cultivate strong home and family relationships. They are natural nurturers, and others seek them out because they feel supported in their presence. In business, they create a supportive community among their customers or clients that fosters loyalty and long-term connections. Sixes bring natural skills in living responsibly – at home and at work. They actually perform a kind of healing in doing this and give comfort to those in need. Their task in life is to learn to be truly helpful to others, and not just a sympathetic ear.

Selfless and service-oriented, one of the challenges of the 6 is to avoid over-giving and people-pleasing/co-dependency. They are born counselors/coaches, and seek to balance their home and work life. Family is very important to them, and they will defend their family vigorously. They need to be careful not to be overly self-sacrificing for the sake of those with whose care they are charged.

The soul's agenda for the 6 is to serve through nurturing their family, their friends, and as entrepreneurs, their tribe or community. They love beauty in all forms – including their home, office and surroundings – and use this love to create harmony in their life. Sixes are highly creative, especially in art, music, and other areas, and are natural counselors and healers. It is the most balanced of all the numbers.

VARIATIONS ON THE INSPIRED SUCCESS PATH 6

6-1: A 6 Life Path with a 1 Expression will want to apply their natural nurturing abilities in a way that involves leadership. They might head up a counseling firm or government agency that serves children, society, the disadvantaged, or animals. They might become executive director of a nonprofit foundation with a similar focus. Stepping into leadership as a 6 requires courage, taking the initiative, being original, innovative, and taking charge – which can be difficult for the 6 with their caretaking tendencies.

6-2: A 6 Life Path with a 2 Expression will want to apply their natural nurturing abilities in an industry and role that values collaboration, teamwork and harmony. The 6 and the 2 (peacemaker) can be compatible energies, but both are prone to co-dependency, so healthy personal boundaries will be key for this type. They will usually want to work with others, rather than alone, and to seek the balanced solution to any issues. They are the "power behind the throne," and rarely want to be in the spotlight.

6-3: A 6 Life Path with a 3 Expression will want to apply their natural nurturing abilities in an industry and role that involves creative arts, communication, or the media. These people are optimistic and upbeat and great storytellers. They are the center of their social circle, and others will tend to come to them to share their problems and get advice, as well as to bring their enthusiastic energy to the gatherings they attend. They can be scattered, so need to learn to focus their interests in one main area.

6-4: A 6 Life Path with a 4 Expression will want to apply their natural nurturing abilities through an industry and role that requires or values organization and structure. Many social service and creative arts organizations – which naturally attract people who are creative and may be less structured – can benefit from having a 6-4 on their team to create the policies, procedures, and plans the firm will need to provide its services. They can see how things fit together better than any other type, but may need a nudge to think "outside of the box."

6-5: A 6 Life Path with a 5 Expression will want to apply their natural nurturing abilities through an industry and role that involves change, travel, and autonomy. They might be itinerant medical service providers, travel agents, international relations experts, politicians, or even ministers. They are excellent communicators, and their biggest challenge is to avoid pursuing new experiences to such an extent that they lack focus when it is needed.

6-6: A 6 Life Path with a 6 Expression has the dual 6 energy, which intensifies both the positive and negative aspects of that energy. Codependency will likely be an area to learn about and avoid for the 6-6! They will want to apply their natural nurturing abilities through an industry and role that involves aesthetic beauty, a sense of family and connectedness, interior design, child care, animal care, or plants. 6-6's love people, and bring a nurturing presence with them wherever they go. They will naturally gravitate to a natural nurturing role within the organizations, foundations or companies that address these areas.

6-7: A 6 Life Path with a 7 Expression will want to apply their natural nurturing abilities through an industry and role that gives them time and space to reflect, analyze and research. Working in a school, research firm, or medical facility would be a great fit for 6-7. They love to delve deeply into a topic and learn all they can about it. 6-7's can also be drawn to metaphysical and spiritual roles and are often intuitive or psychic.

6-8: A 6 Life Path with an 8 Expression will want to apply their natural nurturing abilities through an industry and role that gives them authority and power, values financial gain, and allows them to activate their potential for greatness. They will be naturally successful in business and financial affairs, and are great planners. They may go through ups and downs to reach their desired success, but eventually they will get there, if they avoid seeking money for its own sake.

6-9: A 6 Life Path with a 9 Expression will want to apply their natural nurturing abilities through an industry and role that makes the world a better place. The 6-9 is a humanitarian and/or philanthropist, and leading a nonprofit – or charitable activities of a for-profit firm – is a great fit for them. They also often gravitate to working within theater, music, social services or artistic organizations – or even churches.

6-11: A 6 Life Path with an 11 Expression will want to apply their natural nurturing abilities through an industry and role that connects the seen with the unseen, the conscious with the unconscious. They are spiritual illuminators that often feel different from others, and need to find the place they fit in. They are natural teachers and may find themselves working in training, education or other teaching-related organizations.

6-22: A 6 Life Path with a 22 Expression will want to apply their natural nurturing abilities through an industry and role that offers a global shift and structure – or even builds something brand new. 6-22's have a huge vision for how to improve things, and as the Master Builder bringing the natural nurturing abilities energy of the 6 multiplies the potential impact the 6-22 can have on the world.

EXPRESSION AND SUPPRESSION OF THE INSPIRED SUCCESS PATH 6

Each Inspired Success Path can be either expressed or suppressed, depending on whether the person is working it positively or negatively. Following are the signs of both and what to do if your Path is the 6 and you have begun to suppress your gifts.

Inspired Success Path 6 Expressed

Expressive 6's have learned to channel their desire to serve and care for others into channels that are meaningful for them, while maintaining healthy boundaries around themselves and their relationships. They may be nurturing directly in a helping profession or simply bring their caring essence to a traditional business position.

But they skillfully balance work and family, preserving long-term relationships with friends and coworkers. They use their business savvy to enjoy financial success and widespread impact, helping to solve societal or environmental problems. They create beautiful surroundings in their office and home, and have a healthy respect for responsibility while not being overly perfectionistic.

Inspired Success Path 6 Suppressed

When 6's feel blocked, they will become co-dependent and over-giving to the extent that they become personally depleted and drained, feeling like they have become invisible. They sacrifice themselves for others, and become resentful that others don't do more for them. They may isolate and "pout" as a result. They have a misplaced sense of responsibility, taking on others' responsibilities as though they were their own. This makes them hyper-vigilant, sensitive to the smallest hint of a need of someone within their sphere. They can also become obsessive about following the rules that fall within this perceived responsibility, which in turn depletes their energy and focus.

To get unblocked, the questions to ask are: "What are my true responsibilities now?" or "How can I nurture myself while caring for others now?"

JOBS OR BUSINESSES BEST SUITED TO THE INSPIRED SUCCESS PATH 6

Knowing that the 6, the Nurturing Community Builder, must be in a nurturing, caring role, following are some of the roles they are well suited for:

- Social service

- Counseling or coaching

- Nonprofit foundation or government outreach

- Religious organizations

- Medical roles

- Acting, singing, artist, gardener, landscaper

- Architect

- Athlete

- Interior decorator

- Hair stylist

6 8 4
2 1 5 7
9 1 3 7
0 3

9

INSPIRED SUCCESS PATH 7: THE TALENTED ANALYST OR THE INTUITIVE

Carol, an Inspired Success Path 7-1, was viewed as a "nerd" growing up. She had glasses by the time she was 8 years old, and spent all of her spare time reading. Science and math were her favorite subjects, and she loved doing research projects and lab experiments to discover what works and what doesn't. She majored in pre-med subjects in college, and became a medical research assistant when she graduated. That put her right in the heart of the lab every day, doing experiments and research and writing reports...her sweet spot! She didn't marry – or even date much – because Carol was very introverted and shy and preferred her own company.

She came to me in mid-career, sharing that she had spent the past 5 years going to spiritual retreats and seminars to try to understand the strange sensations she had been getting in her hands. Carol had begun pursuing energy medicine and studying the chakras, and felt drawn to try doing hands-on healing. As I encouraged her to pursue that in a low-risk setting, the results she got with her healing group participants were amazing. She continued following her intuitive guidance and developed a healing method that drew global recognition and led to her writing a book and starting a healing school to teach others how to do it.

TRAITS OF THE INSPIRED SUCCESS PATH 7

Carol's path reflects both the linear and the spiritual side of the 7 Life Path energy. On the one hand, the 7 Life Path brings natural talents in research, analysis, and intellectual pursuits. And on the other, it includes – either from the beginning or as an evolution in mid-career – pursuit of spiritual and metaphysical studies. They tend to analyze everything – including the meaning of existence! – and are on a relentless exploration of the deeper meaning of their life. They are born seekers, and others seek them out for their wisdom. In fact, they often become teachers, professors, researchers, speakers or trainers for this reason. They want to be sure all the facts, citations, and assumptions are correct before they share what they have learned.

They can be quite intuitive – even psychic – as Carol discovered in her mid-career transition. They enjoy solitude, and will go deeply into whatever subject is of interest to them. They require significant alone time to study, analyze and integrate the information they have read. They need to learn to balance solitude and privacy with social interaction to have a balanced life. Their challenge is to maintain their independence without feeling isolated or ineffectual.

It can be hard for the 7 to know when "enough is enough" when it comes to seeking more information. A trap for the 7 is to see him/ herself as the center of the universe and become egocentric. Social contact tempers this. The weakness of the Seven can be being perceived as distant or aloof (perhaps because they are lost in thought). They are well suited to any occupation or business that values research, learning and analysis – or intuition and spiritual insights.

VARIATIONS ON THE INSPIRED SUCCESS PATH 7

7-1: A 7 Life Path with a 1 Expression will want to apply their analytical and/or intuitive abilities in a leadership capacity – perhaps pioneering a new industry, product or service; starting their own business to meet an unmet need in the market; or leading a new technology firm that is blazing new ground. This requires courage, taking the initiative, being original, innovative, and taking charge. The 7-1 will feel conflict if their leadership role requires them to be in public and visible on a regular basis, as they require a great deal of solitude. Being the discoverer or lead on paper, in journal articles, or among industry peers will fulfill their respective needs for research and discovery as well as leadership. If they are spiritually inclined, any religious leadership role should be taken on in partnership with someone who is more extroverted than they are.

7-2: A 7 Life Path with a 2 Expression will want to apply their analytical and/or intuitive abilities in an industry and role that values collaboration, teamwork and harmony. They may actively mediate or negotiate – whether in politics, real estate or business - or they may comfort and soothe people in a counseling or customer service role. They will usually want to work with others, rather than alone, and to seek the balanced solution to any issues. Both the 7 and the 2 seek to be behind the scenes, rather than in the limelight: the 7 wants solitude to research, think and meditate; the 2 wants to be the power behind the leader they support.

7-3: A 7 Life Path with a 3 Expression will want to apply their analytical and/or intuitive abilities in an industry and role that involves creative arts, communication, or the media. These people are optimistic and upbeat and great storytellers. Once they complete their research, they will want to communicate and share what they have discovered, thanks to the creative communication desire the 3 Expression brings. They can be pioneers of entire new industries and inventions – and they want the world to know! The 3 energy can be scattered, so need to learn to focus their interests in one main area.

7-4: A 7 Life Path with a 4 Expression will want to apply their analytical and/or intuitive abilities through an industry and role that requires or values organization and structure. The 7 will research and analyze; they will share the results of that process (and the process itself) through building something lasting and creating structures, policies and procedures to support the analysis. They are drawn to such fields as accounting, finance, law, and operations management, as well as classical music and literature. They can see how things fit together better than any other type, but may feel challenged to think "outside of the box."

7-5: A 7 Life Path with a 5 Expression will want to apply their analytical and/or intuitive abilities through an industry and role that involves change, travel, and autonomy. The 7-5 can be more susceptible to addictions than many other types, since as the 7 seeks solitude yet the 5 quests for new experiences and altered states of consciousness, addictive substances can be quite appealing. 7-5's will explore how their spiritual gifts or research studies could be used to foster change, and their own life may be filled with frequently changing circumstances to help them develop the ability to adapt. They are excellent communicators, and their biggest challenge is to avoid pursuing new experiences to such an extent that they lack focus when it is needed.

7-6: A 7 Life Path with a 6 Expression will want to apply their analytical and/or intuitive abilities through an industry and role that involves aesthetic beauty, a sense of family and connectedness, interior design, child care, animal care, or plants. 7-6's love people, and bring a nurturing presence with them wherever they go. They will naturally gravitate to analytical and/or intuitive roles within the organizations, foundations or companies that address these areas. If they are psychically or intuitively talented, they may bring a combination of spiritual and traditional healing gifts to their clients or patients.

7-7: A 7 Life Path with a 7 Expression has dual 7 energy, which intensifies both the positive and negative aspects of that energy. 7-7's will want to apply their analytical and/or intuitive abilities through an industry and role that gives them ample time and space to reflect, analyze and research. Working in a think tank or scientific/medical research firm would be a great fit for 7-7. They love to delve deeply into a topic and learn all they can about it. 7-7's can have powerful intuitive or psychic gifts, and if so will need to learn how to channel them into a business or profession that leverages them.

7-8: A 7 Life Path with an 8 Expression will want to apply their analytical and/or intuitive abilities through an industry and role that gives them authority and power, values financial gain, and allows them to activate their potential for greatness. They will be naturally successful in business and financial affairs, and are great planners. They may go through ups and downs to reach their desired success, but eventually they will get there, if they avoid seeking money for its own sake.

7-9: A 7 Life Path with a 9 Expression will want to apply their analytical and/or intuitive abilities through an industry and role that makes the world a better place. The 7-9 is a humanitarian and/or philanthropist, and leading a nonprofit – or charitable activities of a for-profit firm – is a great fit for them. They also often gravitate to doing analysis, research or related work in theater, music, or artistic organizations.

7-11: A 7 Life Path with an 11 Expression will want to apply their analytical and/or intuitive abilities through an industry and role that connects the seen with the unseen, the conscious with the unconscious. They are spiritual illuminators that often feel different from others, and need to find the place they fit in. They are natural teachers and may find themselves working in training, education or other teaching-related organizations.

7-22: A 7 Life Path with a 22 Expression will want to apply their analytical and/or intuitive abilities through an industry and role that offers a global shift and structure – or even builds something brand new. 7-22's have a huge vision for how to improve things, and as the Master Builder bringing the analytical and/or intuitive abilities energy of the 1 multiplies the potential impact the 7-22 can have on the world.

EXPRESSION AND SUPPRESSION OF THE INSPIRED SUCCESS PATH 7

Each Inspired Success Path can be either expressed or suppressed, depending on whether the person is working it positively or negatively. Following are the signs of both and what to do if your Path is the 7 and you have begun to suppress your gifts.

Inspired Success Path 7 Expressed

Expressive 7's have designed their lifestyle and work to allow for ample solitude – without feeling isolated or lonely. They feel that their research, analysis and deep thinking capabilities are needed, well appreciated and rewarded through the work they do. Or if they have activated the intuitive/psychic side of the 7 energy, they are actively using their gifts in a healing, intuitive reading, or similar capacity and others are benefiting from their talent. 7's engage in ongoing learning, challenging their boundaries of what they know. They use their sharp minds for worthwhile pursuits, and when they do socialize, they speak effusively about the subjects in which they are interested. They have colleagues – and, if married, a spouse – who understands and respects their need for alone time and allows them the space they need.

Inspired Success Path 7 Suppressed

When 7's feel blocked, they will isolate unduly and feel like no one understands them. They may become critical and demand proof for what is being told to them. They are disconnected from their emotions and as a result focus unduly on concepts, ideas and principles versus people and values. They shy away from dating and close relationships, fearing that may cut into their alone time. They also become selfish and egocentric, believing the world revolves around them. In addition, they may speak from a position of being "high and mighty," using scholarly or technical language, or other terms others can't understand. When the intuitive/psychic 7 energy makes its entrance, suppressed 7's may feel weird, different, and unbalanced as they try to bring these new insights within their sphere of knowledge and familiarity.

To get unblocked, the questions to ask are: "What do I want to study or analyze now?" or "What intuitive insights have I been avoiding?"

JOBS OR BUSINESSES BEST SUITED TO THE INSPIRED SUCCESS PATH 7

Knowing that the 7, the Talented Analyst or Intuitive, must be in an analytical or intuitive/spiritual role, following are some of the roles they are well suited for:

- Entrepreneur (any type) because it allows them autonomy and a platform for their ideas and inventions to be shared

- Scientist/researcher/astronomer

- Physician/dentist

- Investigator

- University professor or academic researcher

- Think tank
- Psychic
- Numerologist
- Astrologer
- Energy healer
- Mathematics
- Lawyer
- Accountant, bookkeeper

10

INSPIRED SUCCESS PATH 8: THE CAPABLE FINANCIAL MANAGER

Susan, an Inspired Success Path 8-8, was born into a well-to-do family who had lived in New York for four generations. Her parents raised her with a keen awareness of money and investments, and she even had her own part-time babysitting jobs to generate spending money, and collected rare coins from the time she was in junior high school. She majored in business and got her M.B.A. degree, and after college went to work for a global management consulting firm. Using her incredible business insights and money-making strategies shared with the clients, Susan rapidly progressed through the ranks and was appointed to be the primary contact for the firm's Fortune 50 clients at the record young age of 25.

Once she married, the international travel became grueling and she sought to make a career change. Real estate seemed like the perfect field to transition into, since she had exceptional people skills and the "Midas touch" when it came to money. She began in traditional real estate, but her firm was the victim of embezzlement and dissolved just a couple of years after she joined it. She knew she had to rebuild her career, and since the housing bubble had just burst, she cashed in on the short sale market. By forming her own firm and staffing it as a "one-stop shop" for people needing to do short sales – as well as aligning with several major lenders who wanted to offload their book of business – she captured the lion's share of the New York market for short sales and sold the firm for $10 million before she was 40.

TRAITS OF THE INSPIRED SUCCESS PATH 8

Susan's story is not only of the 8 Life Path, but the dual energy of that life path with an 8 Expression – twice the success, twice the cash! And a major setback is often part of the path – but amazingly, the 8 will have regained the wealth they lost within a relatively short time following such a setback. The primary areas in which the 8 Life Path excels are finances, power, and business. 8's are natural leaders – and business success comes easily to them (albeit with the occasional setback). They are dynamic individuals, understand the material world and intuitively know what makes a company work. They are "take-charge" people, and are best placed when their role involves the bigger picture, vision and strategy, as well as long-term goals, such as CEO, CFO, or owner of their own firm that helps many people in a worthwhile way.

Others will look to the 8 when a decision needs to be made. 8's typically leave a legacy – which if not financial will be a legacy of accomplishment. People on this path have relatively little time for dreams and visions, as they are busy applying their instinctive organizational abilities to the real world. Eights are usually confident, charismatic individuals who are adept at spotting trends and opportunities. Their challenge is learning to manipulate money and power without becoming corrupted or self-seeking in the process.

The 8 needs to achieve a high degree of detachment, understanding that power and influence must be used for the benefit of mankind. Otherwise, they could lose it all – and gain it back again – which as we saw above, they do with relative ease.

8's are intended to have a position of power and dominion over some part of the earth – a company, family, community or other entity. Money and authority are both available to the Eight if they use their discipline and perseverance to reach the goal. And they often face many obstacles. They naturally understand money, authority and power and can work doggedly toward important goals. They key to their success is balancing their higher ideals with reality, the material with the spiritual.

VARIATIONS ON THE INSPIRED SUCCESS PATH 8

8-1: An 8 Life Path with a 1 Expression will want to apply their business and financial abilities in a leadership capacity – perhaps pioneering a new industry, or segment thereof; starting their own business to meet an unmet need in the market; or leading a start-up. The 8 will need to draw on his/her requires courage, taking the initiative, being original, innovative, and taking charge. (Even if it feels scary at times!) The 8-1's talents include originality, creativity and the ability to launch plans into motion.

8-2: An 8 Life Path with a 2 Expression will want to apply their business and financial abilities in an industry and role that values collaboration, teamwork and harmony. They may actively mediate or negotiate – whether in politics, real estate or business - or they may comfort and soothe people in a counseling or customer service role. They will usually want to work with others, rather than alone, and to seek the balanced solution to any issues. They may feel some internal conflict between their business skills and the natural desire of the 2 Expression to be "behind the scenes."

8-3: An 8 Life Path with a 3 Expression will want to apply their business and financial abilities in an industry and role that involves creative arts, communication, or the media. These people are optimistic and upbeat and great storytellers. They are the center of their social circle, and can use their communication skills combined with their business savvy to market, sell, persuade and influence leaders and audiences with ease. They can be scattered, so need to learn to focus their interests in one main area.

8-4: An 8 Life Path with a 4 Expression will want to apply their business and financial abilities through an industry and role that requires or values organization and structure – perhaps one that is in a bit of chaos when this person arrives! They are drawn to such fields as accounting, finance, law, and operations management, as well as classical music and literature. They can see how things fit together better than any other type, especially when it comes to business systems and structures. They can excel in fields that involve large-scale projects such as operations, finance, construction and more.

8-5: An 8 Life Path with a 5 Expression will want to apply their business and financial abilities through an industry and role that involves change, travel, and autonomy. They might be sales managers, executives in the travel industry, ambassadors or international relations experts, politicians, or turnaround experts. They are excellent communicators, and their biggest challenge is to avoid pursuing new experiences to such an extent that they lack focus when it is needed.

8-6: An 8 Life Path with a 6 Expression will want to apply their business and financial abilities through an industry and role that involves aesthetic beauty, a sense of family and connectedness, interior design, child care, animal care, or plants. 8-6's love people, and bring a nurturing presence with them wherever they go. They will naturally gravitate to a business, leadership or financial role within the organizations, foundations or companies that address these areas.

8-7: An 8 Life Path with a 7 Expression will want to apply their business and financial abilities through an industry and role that gives them time and space to reflect, analyze and research. Working in a leadership role in a think tank, scientific/medical research firm or university setting – including educational administration - would be a great fit for 8-7. They love to delve deeply into a topic and learn all they can about it. 8-7's can also be drawn to metaphysical and spiritual roles and are often intuitive or psychic.

8-8: An 8 Life Path with an 8 Expression has dual 8 energy, like Susan whom we met above, which intensifies both the positive and negative aspects of that energy. They are almost guaranteed both financial and business success and that they will need to rebuild after an unexpected setback at least once. They will want to apply their business and financial abilities through an industry and role that gives them authority and power, values financial gain, and allows them to activate their potential for greatness. They may go through ups and downs to reach their desired success, but eventually they will get there, if they avoid seeking money for its own sake.

8-9: An 8 Life Path with a 9 Expression will want to apply their business and financial abilities through an industry and role that makes the world a better place. The 8-9 is a humanitarian and/or philanthropist, and leading a nonprofit – or charitable activities of a for-profit firm – is a great fit for them. They also often gravitate to leading theater, music, or artistic organizations.

8-11: An 8 Life Path with an 11 Expression will want to apply their business and financial abilities through an industry and role that connects the seen with the unseen, the conscious with the unconscious. They are spiritual illuminators that often feel different from others, and need to find the place they fit in. They are natural teachers and may find themselves leading training, education or other teaching-related organizations.

8-22: An 8 Life Path with a 22 Expression will want to apply their business and financial abilities through an industry and role that offers a global shift and structure – or even builds something brand new. 8-22's have a huge vision for how to improve things, and as the Master Builder bringing the business and financial abilities energy of the 1 multiplies the potential impact the 8-22 can have on the world.

EXPRESSION AND SUPPRESSION OF THE INSPIRED SUCCESS PATH 8

Each Inspired Success Path can be either expressed or suppressed, depending on whether the person is working it positively or negatively. Following are the signs of both and what to do if your Path is the 8 and you have begun to suppress your gifts.

Inspired Success Path 8 Expressed

Expressive 8's are business magnates, managing large enterprises (their own or others') with ease. They often become quite wealthy through their business or career activities, and become widely recognized (sometimes even famous) in their field. They are using their ability to create and implement a big vision such that the organization works like a well-oiled machine. Eights may also apply their talents in accomplishments related to pursuits not related to money, such as a charitable foundation or family unit. Expressive 8's have mastered the balance between following money and power for their own sake, and doing it with the greater good in mind.

Inspired Success Path 8 Suppressed

When 8's feel blocked, they can become money-mongers or power-hungry, even authoritarian and dominating in their demeanor and language. They may have issues with money, accumulating debt, avoiding the accumulation of money, or and seeing money and/or power as the ultimate goal. They may have major setbacks that are difficult – sometimes even impossible – to bounce back from. They may misuse the power that comes naturally to them, taking advantage of others or using them on their way to the top. This can, of course, repel people from them, and leave them feeling alone with their control issues.

To get unstuck, the questions to ask include: "What do I want to lead now?" or "How can I make money with this idea now?"

JOBS OR BUSINESSES BEST SUITED TO THE INSPIRED SUCCESS PATH 8

Knowing that the 8, the Capable Financial Manager, must be in a business leadership role, following are some of the roles they are well suited for:

- Entrepreneur (any type) because it lets them carve their own course

- Educational administration

- Operations management

- CEO

- CFO

- Head of entertainment or publishing company

- Government leader

- Real estate or property management

- Hospital administrator

- Any leadership role

- Banker

- Athlete

6 8 4
2 1 5 7
9 0 3

11

INSPIRED SUCCESS PATH 9: THE HUMANITARIAN TRANSFORMER

David, an Inspired Success Path 9-5, came into this world through a difficult premature birth – and his parents were not sure he would survive the incubation period, but he did. As a child he was prone to fantasizing he was an action-hero type, often imagining how he could make the world a better place. When other children were being bullied or left out at school, he would befriend them and reassure them everything would be okay. He would sometimes make up games – including all the rules of the game – and invite other children to play them with him.

He got his college degree in philosophy, and was hired to teach at a university. Almost immediately after he graduated, however, he began volunteering at a local homeless shelter, and soon found himself traveling to Africa to work with the rural villages there to get them water and essential supplies. Being a 5 Expression, he loved the travel and the unpredictable conditions he encountered in his international work. Providing emergency relief following natural disasters was a natural next step, and he soon left the university to work full time with the Red Cross, heading up their relief efforts. He felt like he could better the world in a tangible way through this work.

TRAITS OF THE INSPIRED SUCCESS PATH 9

Those on the 9 Life Path are often destined to travel a humanitarian path. These individuals make great diplomats, environmentalists, veterinarians, teachers, judges, social workers, nuns, priests and healers. They inspire others – through their work and through the example of their life – and are socially conscious, philanthropic, and deeply concerned about the state of the world. This life path is one of universal love, including compassion and tolerance – ultimately leading to work focusing on tolerance and caring for all.

Nines are born healers, whether traditional healing or creative pursuits such as writing or painting. One of the key lessons on the 9 life path is to learn how to let go, and surrender the self for the greater good. Nines can be disappointed by the realities of life: shortcomings of others or of themselves. Money often comes to them through mysterious or unexpected ways. Work with a nonprofit or with a humanitarian component, as David did, is a good fit for the 9.

Nines are the "righter of wrongs" and their deepest intention is to transform the world – so much so that they will sacrifice to advance their cause. They are visionaries and can direct the masses in taking action toward compassionate, transformational initiatives. They will be challenged to stay grounded and communicate within the physical (not just the spiritual or metaphysical) plane, and to surrender their personal good for the greater good of humanity.

VARIATIONS ON THE INSPIRED SUCCESS PATH 9

9-1: A 9 Life Path with a 1 Expression will want to apply their humanitarian gifts in a leadership capacity. They may lead a charitable foundation, a community outreach effort, or similar venture. The essence of what they lead needs to better the world – and they will need to sacrifice their personal good for the good of the whole. This requires courage, taking the initiative, being original, innovative, and taking charge. The 1 Expression requires originality, creativity and launching plans into motion.

9-2: A 9 Life Path with a 2 Expression will want to apply their humanitarian gifts in an industry and role that values collaboration, teamwork and harmony. They may actively mediate or negotiate – whether in a for-profit or non-profit setting – or they may work tirelessly to build support around an issue they care about that will improve the world or mankind. They will usually want to work with others, rather than alone, and to seek the balanced solution to any issues.

9-3: A 9 Life Path with a 3 Expression will want to apply their humanitarian gifts in an industry and role that involves creative arts, communication, or the media. These people are optimistic and upbeat and great storytellers. They are sought after for their wisdom and higher perspective on issues, and others will come to them when they want a visionary to rally support or to see beyond the current limited viewpoint. They can be scattered, so need to learn to focus their interests in one main area.

9-4: A 9 Life Path with a 4 Expression will want to apply their humanitarian gifts through an industry and role that requires or values organization and structure. They may be the director of the charity or arts organization that provides the framework, structure and rules by which to operate. They are drawn to such fields as accounting, finance, law, and operations management, as well as classical music and literature – but need to see how their core discipline helps improve the world in order to feel fulfilled. They can see how things fit together better than any other type, but may need a nudge to bend the rules when necessary.

9-5: A 9 Life Path with a 5 Expression will want to apply their humanitarian gifts through an industry and role that involves change, travel, and autonomy. They might be international relations experts, politicians, or government officials. They are excellent communicators, and their biggest challenge is to avoid pursuing new experiences to such an extent that they lack focus when it is needed.

9-6: A 9 Life Path with a 6 Expression will want to apply their humanitarian gifts through an industry and role that involves aesthetic beauty, a sense of family and connectedness, interior design, child care, animal care, or plants. 1-6's love people, and bring a nurturing presence with them wherever they go. They will naturally gravitate to a humanitarian roles within the organizations, foundations or companies that address these areas.

9-7: A 9 Life Path with a 7 Expression will want to apply their humanitarian gifts through an industry and role that gives them time and space to reflect, analyze and research. Working in a think tank or scientific/medical research firm focusing on humanitarian aid, new science to streamline cures to diseases, and the like would be a great fit for 9-7. They love to delve deeply into a topic and learn all they can about it. 9-7's can also be drawn to metaphysical and spiritual roles and are often intuitive or psychic.

9-8: A 9 Life Path with an 8 Expression will want to apply their humanitarian gifts through an industry and role that gives them authority and power, values financial gain, and allows them to activate their potential for greatness. They will be naturally successful in business and financial affairs, and are great planners. They may go through ups and downs to reach their desired success, but eventually they will get there, if they avoid seeking money for its own sake.

9-9: A 9 Life Path with a 9 Expression has dual 9 energy, which intensifies both the positive and negative aspects of that energy. This will make it all the more difficult for them to feel like they fit on planet Earth. They will be drawn apply their humanitarian gifts through an industry and role that makes the world a better place. The 9-9 is the consummate humanitarian and/or philanthropist, and leading a nonprofit — or charitable activities of a for-profit firm — is a great fit for them. They also often gravitate to leading theater, music, or artistic organizations.

9-11: A 9 Life Path with an 11 Expression will want to apply their humanitarian gifts through an industry and role that connects the seen with the unseen, the conscious with the unconscious. They are spiritual illuminators that often feel different from others, and need to find the place they fit in. They are natural teachers and may find themselves leading training, education or other teaching-related organizations.

9-22: A 9 Life Path with a 22 Expression will want to apply their humanitarian gifts through an industry and role that offers a global shift and structure — or even builds something brand new. 9-22's have a huge vision for how to improve things, and as the Master Builder bringing the humanitarian gifts energy of the 9 multiplies the potential impact the 9-22 can have on the world.

EXPRESSION AND SUPPRESSION OF THE INSPIRED SUCCESS PATH 9

Each Inspired Success Path can be either expressed or suppressed, depending on whether the person is working it positively or negatively. Following are the signs of both and what to do if your Path is the 9 and you have begun to suppress your gifts.

Inspired Success Path 9 Expressed

Expressive 9's are fulfilling their internal drive to make the world a better place by working in a career that is service-oriented. They teach by example how to live in a selfless way. And although they may still have moments of not feeling like they belong on the planet, for the most part they believe they are on course with their calling and contributing in the ways they can. They may also volunteer in the community or for charitable causes if their work is not directly involved in those areas. They have learned not to be unduly affected by the inevitable disappointments in the daily realities of life. Expressive 9's use the ever-present connection with the Divine they feel to provide insights and wisdom for them as they face dilemmas and challenges in life. They leave a legacy of transformation and improvement, regardless of their chosen endeavor.

Inspired Success Path 9 Suppressed

When 9's feel blocked, they will often become moody, withdrawn, even aloof as they withdraw into themselves, feeling like "I don't fit here." They can be quite esoteric in their speech and outlook, such that others have a hard time understanding what they are talking about. They may even begin to mistake their own wisdom for God's wisdom and become zealous about their beliefs. Unusual diseases or illnesses may plague the suppressed 9 until they become clear on how to focus their broad vision and perspective in the physical dimension.

To get unblocked, the questions to ask are: "What do I want to improve now?" or "Where do I want to give of my time, talents or money now?"

JOBS OR BUSINESSES BEST SUITED TO THE INSPIRED SUCCESS PATH 9

Knowing that the 9, the Humanitarian Transformer, must be in a humanitarian role, following are some of the roles they are well suited for:

- University professor or teacher in any context
- Charitable foundation director
- Entertainment – especially science fiction or metaphysical genres
- Government or community outreach roles
- Minister/nun/priest
- Politician
- Lawyer
- Photographer
- Environmentalist
- Diplomat
- Veterinarian
- Teacher
- Judge
- Healer

$$6 \quad 8 \quad 4$$
$$2 \quad 1 \quad 5 \quad 7$$
$$9 \quad 0 \quad 3 \quad 7$$

12

MASTER INSPIRED
SUCCESS PATH 11:
THE SPIRITUAL MESSENGER

Desiree, an Inspired Success Path 11-7, was raised in Europe in a family to whom spirituality was discussed daily. They were aware of angels and invisible personal guides, and each member of the family was encouraged to dialog with his/her guides regularly. She studied each of the archangels and guides and learned their names, their characteristics, the areas in which each helped people, and various ways to contact them. Desiree didn't know that talking with (and being aware of) your guides was unusual until she moved to the U.S. to attend college – and people didn't understand this strange concept at all! But they were intrigued, and she began holding weekly meetings to help interested students connect with their spiritual guides. She had a natural ability to teach and facilitate this connection, and found her groups growing quickly.

Finally, she decided to record some of her sessions and write a guidebook on how to connect to your guides. It was immediately picked up by a leading spiritual publisher and she found herself speaking to large audiences of spiritual seekers before she knew it!

WHAT MASTER NUMBERS ARE

Most numbers are reduced to a single digit when calculating the numerology profile. However, when we get a total of 11 or 22, they are not reduced, because they are "Master Numbers." These Master Numbers have special qualities to them, and are seen to have more potential in their energy than the other single-digit numbers. But don't get the wrong idea! Master numbers, while having increased potential, also bring an increased level of responsibility with them. They require time, maturity – often an "old soul" – and effort to integrate this powerful, high-vibration energy into one's human experience. (Note that the 33 is also considered a Master Number but is so rare that we will not discuss it here.)

As numerologists, we believe that the souls who choose Master Numbers to be in their core numbers (such as the Life Path and the Expression) have made a pre-birth contract to serve humanity in a conscious way in this lifetime. And at the same time, it helps the person who has that Master Number also learn and evolve on their own spiritual path.

People with Master Numbers in their profile have the potential for greater spiritual sensitivities than people with single digit numbers. Their life may feel like a series of tests designed to hone these innate abilities. However, they may or may not feel up to the challenge of connecting to and expressing this energy. If they don't, they will experience that aspect of their profile at the vibration of the single digit that represents the sum of the master number digits. For example, the 11 who is not yet ready to be the Spiritual Messenger would vibrate and act like a 2 (1 + 1 = 2), and a 22 would vibrate at the level of the 4 (2 + 2 = 4).

TRAITS OF THE MASTER INSPIRED SUCCESS PATH 11

The 11/2 Life Path is the most intuitive of all the numbers. People on this path are blessed with the ability illuminate mankind spiritually. Often misunderstood early in life, 11's may become shy and withdrawn – but they have more potential than they know. They are a channel for information between the higher and lower worlds – and indeed can invent new technology, objects and cures for diseases using their insights from the higher dimension.

With this intense energy available to them, 11's will engage in a great deal of self-reflection, and may feel self-conscious. They must do their personal growth and other inner work to be fully ready to deliver the transformational message with which they have been entrusted. In the meantime, they may wonder what they are really here to do, they may feel confused, and even criticize themselves for not fitting into the crowd.

Once the 11 is ready to start sharing their spiritual message, they naturally take to the stage and love being in the spotlight. They may do spontaneous readings from the stage, passionately share a vision of a brighter future, or channel inspired content from within. And people are drawn to them in droves – not necessarily knowing why.

The 11 soul's agenda is to inspire and uplift – but they may find that they teeter between their call to greatness and spiritual insight, and self-destructive tendencies if they shy away from their calling. 11's are often old souls who are here to accept and live up to their destiny and use their creativity and intuitive abilities for the good of humanity. They are transformers, reformers, and change agents. Like a lightning rod, they attract powerful ideas, even psychic impressions. They have a powerful presence and have the inherent ability to conduct the higher vibrations – if they are willing!

VARIATIONS ON THE INSPIRED SUCCESS PATH 11

11-1: 11 Life Paths with a 1 Expression will want to apply their spiritual illumination abilities in a leadership capacity. And given the spiritual nature of their message, they may have to summon their courage, take the initiative, and be willing to share what might be perceived as weird, esoteric or unconventional. But as their ideas become more widely accepted and proven, they will be seen as the wise sage who pioneered a movement. Their talents include originality, creativity and the ability to find spiritual solutions to global problems.

11-2: 11 Life Paths with a 2 Expression will want to apply their spiritual illumination abilities in an industry and role that values collaboration, teamwork and harmony. They may encourage collaboration among people with opposing positions, or they may simply help individuals resolve the internal conflicting dialogs among their mind, body, emotions and soul. They will usually want to work with others, rather than alone, and to seek the balanced solution to any issues. Partnerships with other spiritually-minded people help them summon the courage they need to share their gifts.

11-3: 11 Life Paths with a 3 Expression will want to apply their spiritual illumination abilities in an industry and role that involves creative arts, communication, or the media. These people are optimistic and upbeat and great storytellers. They are the center of their social circle, since they are both charismatic and persuasive communicators. 11-3's are able to see the deeper meaning in the issues in many conversations, so their perspective is highly valued in decision-making, planning, and obtaining guidance. They can be scattered, so need to learn to focus their interests in one main area.

11-4: 11 Life Paths with a 4 Expression will want to apply their spiritual illumination abilities through an industry and role that requires or values organization and structure – perhaps one that is in a bit of chaos when this person arrives! They are drawn to such fields as accounting, finance, law, and operations management, as well as classical music and literature. They can see how things fit together better than any other type, but may need encouragement to bend the rules as they share their new ideas.

11-5: 11 Life Paths with a 5 Expression will want to apply their spiritual illumination abilities through an industry and role that involves change, travel, and autonomy. They might decide to take their "ministry" (whether formal or not) on the road and share live seminars on an itinerant basis. They seek to bring spiritual insights into the areas that are ready to receive them, so the life of the 11-5 can be exciting and unpredictable as they listen to their internal guidance about where to share their message now and follow it. They are excellent communicators, and their biggest challenge is to avoid pursuing new experiences to such an extent that they lack focus when it is needed.

11-6: 11 Life Paths with a 6 Expression will want to apply their spiritual illumination abilities through an industry and role that involves aesthetic beauty, a sense of family and connectedness, interior design, child care, animal care, or plants. 11-6's love people, and bring a nurturing presence with them wherever they go. They will naturally gravitate to roles within churches, foundations, organizations, or companies that address these areas.

11-7: 11 Life Paths with a 7 Expression will want to apply their spiritual illumination abilities through an industry and role that gives them time and space to reflect, analyze and research. Delving deeply into spiritual topics such as energy medicine, chakras, alternative medicine, spiritual texts or similar pursuits be a great fit for an 11-7. They love to learn all they can about the topics that interest and call to them. 11-7's can also be drawn to metaphysical and spiritual roles and are usually quite intuitive or psychic.

11-8: 11 Life Paths with an 8 Expression will want to apply their spiritual illumination abilities through an industry and role that gives them authority and power, values financial gain, and allows them to activate their potential for greatness. They will be naturally successful in business and financial affairs, and are great planners. They may go through ups and downs to reach their desired success, but eventually they will get there, if they avoid seeking money for its own sake.

11-9: 11 Life Paths with a 9 Expression will want to apply their spiritual illumination abilities through an industry and role that makes the world a better place. The 11-9 combination is similar to the 11-11 in that both numbers are highly focused on humanitarianism. So roles as a philanthropist, leading a nonprofit – or the charitable activities of a for-profit firm – are examples of good careers for them. They also often gravitate to leading theater, music, or artistic organizations.

11-11: 11 Life Paths with an 11 Expression has dual 11 energy, which intensifies both the positive and negative aspects of that energy. They will want to apply their spiritual illumination abilities through an industry and role that connects the seen with the unseen, the conscious with the unconscious. They are master spiritual illuminators that often feel different from others, and need to find the place they fit in. They are natural teachers and may find themselves leading training, education or other teaching-related organizations.

11-22: 11 Life Paths with a 22 Expression will want to apply their spiritual illumination abilities through an industry and role that offers a global shift and structure – or even builds something brand new. 11-22's have a huge vision for how to improve things, and as the Master Builder bringing the spiritual illumination abilities energy of the 11 multiplies the potential impact the 11-22 can have on the world.

EXPRESSION AND SUPPRESSION OF THE INSPIRED SUCCESS PATH 11

Each Inspired Success Path can be either expressed or suppressed, depending on whether the person is working it positively or negatively.

Following are the signs of both and what to do if your Path is the 11 and you have begun to suppress your gifts.

Inspired Success Path 11 Expressed

Expressive 11's have reconciled and accepted the high vibration of the spiritual gifts and insights they have been given, and are expressing and using them in their work. They usually find themselves in a teaching role – whether officially or not – and their very presence inspires others and enriches their self-concept as they move through their life. They may be perceived as eccentric by some – as Mozart and DaVinci, both 11/2 Life Paths, were in their time. But their gifts must be expressed!

Until they are ready for the 11 vibration, they may find themselves seemingly content focusing on peacemaking, cooperation, teamwork and facilitating harmony through their work (the lower vibration 2 energy).

Inspired Success Path 11 Suppressed

When 11's feel blocked, they will withdraw, feel like they don't belong on the planet, and will engage in extreme self-doubt. They may even act out in a self-destructive way in an attempt to resist the 11 energy that calls to them. They may disregard their intuition and feel like they have lost their way...but the good news is that the way back to themselves is within them.

To get unblocked, the questions to ask are: "What do I feel led to teach now?" or "What spiritual or intuitive gifts or message is seeking to awaken within me now?"

JOBS OR BUSINESSES BEST SUITED TO THE INSPIRED SUCCESS PATH 11

Knowing that the 11, the Spiritual Messenger, must be in a spiritual illumination role, following are some of the roles they are well suited for:

- Healer
- Psychic
- Intuitive
- Inventor
- Musician
- Speaker
- Teacher
- Minister
- Writer
- Astrologer
- Numerologist

$$26^{84}_{2}1^{57}_{9}0^{37}_{3}$$

13

MASTER INSPIRED SUCCESS PATH 22: THE MASTER BUILDER

James, an Inspired Success Path 22-6, was always mechanically inclined. From assembling Legos® when he was a toddler to building model cars in childhood, he loved knowing how things worked. He began designing his own futuristic car models in the sixth grade, and before long was taking clocks, computers, and other mechanical devices apart to see how they were put together – and how to improve them.

He majored in mechanical engineering in college, and was hired by a technology firm upon graduation. Designing jigs and fixtures for their clean rooms was challenging for him at first, but in his late 30's he began sensing a higher calling on his life. The computer industry growth curve had become flat, and he began to see how combining television, telephone, internet and video gaming into one unit was the future of technology. He played with his idea in his spare time until finally he was ready to present it to his firm. They jumped at the chance to pioneer new technology that could put them on a growth curve once again, and put James in charge of that division of the company.

TRAITS OF THE MASTER INSPIRED SUCCESS PATH 22/4

James' story demonstrates awareness of the 22 Master Builder energy from childhood – and its upleveling to the Master level in his midlife. The 22 is recognized as the most powerful of all the numbers. People on this special path have an extraordinary ability to turn dreams into reality. As the Master Builder, they create activities, programs and structures that benefit humanity. Good planning, management and organizational principles undergird everything they do (since it is a higher vibration of the 4 energy). They may become planners, organizers, statesmen, presidents or executives. They command respect and are seen as experts in their field.

22/4's are very practical in the application of their gifts and talents – even though they may have spiritual direction in the path to their invention or other legacy. They are aware – consciously or subconsciously – of the relatively slow reality of the earth plane as well as the fast-moving world of creativity and raw ideas, where anything is possible at any time. 22's also excel in advancing relationships and helping people come into harmony, since they embody the double energy of the 2.

The 22 soul's agenda is to be a builder of their dreams, and execute plans and projects that will benefit humankind. 22's use spiritual principles to manifest physical structures. Their lessons are around competence and efficiency and lead to magnificent creations. These Master Builders dream big, and want to leave their mark on civilization. Of all the numbers, the 22 has the greatest potential for accomplishment – but also the greatest liability: it will take their entire life to accomplish their big vision.

VARIATIONS ON THE INSPIRED SUCCESS PATH 22

22-1: A 22 Life Path with a 1 Expression will want to apply their Master Builder abilities in a leadership role – perhaps pioneering a new industry, or segment thereof; starting their own business to share a new technology or invention of theirs; or leading an organization that sells a new drug or approach to treating a long-standing disease. This requires courage, taking the initiative, being original, innovative, and taking charge – and it will require the 22-1 to be patient with the process and to stretch along the way!   A 22-1's talents include originality, creativity and the ability to launch big visions and plans into physical action.

22-2: A 22 Life Path with a 2 Expression has, in essence, the triple 2 energy, so their life and work will be filled with people, people, people! They will want to apply their Master Builder abilities in an industry and role that values collaboration, teamwork and harmony. They may actively mediate or negotiate – whether in politics, real estate or business - or they may comfort and advise people in a counseling or customer service role. They will exercise their insights on how to harmonize disparate factions or individuals in new ways.

22-3: A 22 Life Path with a 3 Expression will want to apply their Master Builder abilities in an industry and role that involves creative arts, communication, or the media. These people are optimistic and upbeat and great storytellers. People are amazed at their insights about how to bring together different components of a situation, industry or group and find common ground. The more they can express their ideas through written or spoken words, art or other creative modalities, the bigger impact they can have. They can be scattered, so need to learn to focus their interests in one main area.

22-4: A 22 Life Path with a 4 Expression will want to apply their Master Builder abilities through an industry and role that requires or values organization and structure. Here we again see a dual, intensified energy: 22/4-4. These unique individuals can find order in seeming chaos, and build systems that last in any field, whether science, math, finance, manufacturing or spirituality. They have a knack for seeing how things fit together, but need to be careful not to become too focused on the "black and white" rules – they will need to be modified in some situations.

22-5: A 22 Life Path with a 5 Expression will want to apply their Master Builder abilities through an industry and role that involves change, travel, and autonomy. They might become salespeople, travel agents, international relations experts, politicians, or even ministers. They are excellent communicators, and their biggest challenge is to avoid pursuing new experiences to such an extent that they lack focus when it is needed.

22-6: A 22 Life Path with a 6 Expression will want to apply their Master Builder abilities through an industry and role that involves aesthetic beauty, a sense of family and connectedness, interior design, child care, animal care, or plants. 22-6's love people, and bring a nurturing presence with them wherever they go. They will naturally gravitate to a key role within the organizations, foundations or companies that address these areas.

22-7: A 22 Life Path with a 7 Expression will want to apply their Master Builder abilities through an industry and role that gives them time and space to reflect, analyze and research. Working in a think tank or scientific/medical research firm would be a great fit for 22-7. They love to delve deeply into a topic and learn all they can about it. 22-7's can also be drawn to metaphysical and spiritual roles and are often intuitive or psychic.

22-8: A 22 Life Path with an 8 Expression will want to apply their Master Builder abilities through an industry and role that gives them authority and power, values financial gain, and allows them to activate their potential for greatness. They will be naturally successful in business and financial affairs, and are great planners. They may go through ups and downs to reach their desired success, but eventually they will get there, if they avoid seeking money for its own sake.

22-9: A 22 Life Path with a 9 Expression will want to apply their Master Builder abilities through an industry and role that makes the world a better place. The 22-9 is a humanitarian and/or philanthropist, and leading a nonprofit – or charitable activities of a for-profit firm – is a great fit for them. They also often gravitate to leading theater, music, or artistic organizations.

22-11: A 22 Life Path with an 11 Expression will want to apply their Master Builder abilities through an industry and role that connects the seen with the unseen, the conscious with the unconscious. This is a double master number, so it is not an easy life path! They are spiritual illuminators that often feel different from others, and need to find the place they fit in. They are natural teachers and may find themselves leading training, education or other teaching-related organizations.

22-22: A 22 Life Path with a 22 Expression has dual 22 energy, which intensifies both the positive and negative aspects of that energy. They will want to apply their Master Builder abilities through an industry and role that offers a global shift and structure – or even builds something brand new. 22-22's have a huge vision for how to improve things, and bring the dual Master Builder abilities energy of the 22 which multiplies the potential impact they can have on the world.

EXPRESSION AND SUPPRESSION OF THE INSPIRED SUCCESS PATH 22

Each Inspired Success Path can be either expressed or suppressed, depending on whether the person is working it positively or negatively. Following are the signs of both and what to do if your Path is the 22 and you have begun to suppress your gifts.

Inspired Success Path 22 Expressed

Expressive 22's are engaged in big work in the world! They are exercising their natural gifts in business, systems design, and global transformation in their work – and perhaps also in volunteer activities. They see a way to improve the world with something they can build (with the support and contributions of a team) – and they are setting the structures, plans and systems in place to create that change. But they are not all vision – they have an innate sense of what is practical and what will really work, and they bring that to all phases of the projects in which they are involved.

Until they are fully ready to allow the Master energy of the 22 to come forth, the 22/4 will live through the lower vibration of the 4. They will still act strategically and be able to see how things fit together, but may not sense the full scope of the grand vision that lies within them – until the time is right in their personal growth.

Inspired Success Path 22 Suppressed

When 22's feel blocked, they feel intense pressure from the power of their own vision for improvement. The incredible possibilities can "stop them in their tracks," as they doubt whether others can comprehend – let alone assist them with – their vision. They demonstrate a lack of trust in others, and think they must carry out this huge undertaking alone, when it is in fact so big that many people will need to be involved. They may become workaholic, driven to achieve huge results without getting help. And they may shy away from the spiritual insights that are available to them through the Master number, leading to escape through addictions or overwork in their early life.

To get unblocked, the questions to ask are: "What do I want to build now?" or "What needs to be harmonized now, within me or in this situation?"

JOBS OR BUSINESSES BEST SUITED TO THE INSPIRED SUCCESS PATH 22

Knowing that the 22, the Master Builder, must be in a role that allows them to organize, build and invent, following are some of the roles they are well suited for:

- Architect

- Engineer

- CEO

- Executive Director – Charitable Foundation

- CFO

- COO

- Chief Strategist

- Research & Development Manager

- Diplomat

- School Superintendent

- Government Leader

PART THREE:

THE "OTHER NUMBERS" THAT MAKE YOU UNIQUE

In this Part, we will explore three additional numbers which have a key bearing on your Inspired Success Path and its impact on your business or profession, including:

- Heart's Desire Number
- Birthday Number
- Personality Number
- Maturity Number

684
2 15 7
9 1 3
0

14

YOUR HEART'S DESIRE –
YOUR INNERMOST
YEARNING

After years in financial sales, Sam (whom we met in chapter 7) was
at a crossroads. Although he enjoyed his work, he felt like he had
accomplished as much as he could – and something deeper was
calling to him. He started wondering about the meaning of his life –
and how he could use his talents to help others in a bigger way.

One weekend he was invited to an out-of-state company sales
meeting. When he and the others arrived, they were told that they
would not be presenting or developing sales plans that weekend
– but would be participating in a personal growth training. It was
there that Sam discovered an ancient assessment tool with which he
absolutely resonated. He delved deeply into learning more about
it – and using it with his sales teams – and got amazing results. From
this foundation, he started a life coaching and speaking firm helping
individuals improve their work and personal relationships using this
tool. Shortly afterward, he also began volunteering and served on

the board of a local charity providing art therapy to special needs children – which was incredibly satisfying for him.

What happened to Sam? Why the sudden switch in focus?

Sam had come face to face with his Heart's Desire – which in this case was a 9, the philanthropist and humanitarian. His 5-1 Inspired Success Path had been altered by his inner motivation: the desire to help improve others' lives and the planet in some broad-based way.

There can be other explanations for radical mid-career changes, or for losing interest in what you used to love – including the emergence of your Maturity Number (see chapter 17), a new Pinnacle (see chapter 24) or even just a Personal Year 5, which inherently involves changes. But the Heart's Desire deserves some discussion, since at times it can be dormant and you may be unaware of it – when other times it becomes more dominant than any of the other energies in your profile, and you must heed its needs!

WHAT IS THE HEART'S DESIRE?

The *Heart's Desire number* is what it sounds like: *that which you most desire to accomplish, in your innermost being, as the result of your life.* It is the answer to the question, "If I use the gifts of my Life Path and fully share them through my chosen avenue of Expression, what is the ultimate result?" It is also the outcome of your friendships, family relationships, hobbies, lifestyle and all of who you are.

The Heart's Desire is what makes you happiest and feeds your soul. This number is your inner motivation and tends to influence your decisions and why you choose the things you do. It is also known as the Soul Number. It holds your secret thoughts and wishes and says what you long for, in your heart of hearts.

Whenever you enter into a close personal or business relationship, find out the Heart's Desire of your prospective partner! It will show the essence of who they are, and provide you with insights that transcend skills-based or personality-based assessments. The Expression number depicts the outer expression of the person's gifts, whereas the Heart's Desire shows the inner longing.

The Heart's Desire is derived from adding the energetic vibration of all of just the vowels in your birth name. (Refer to the chart in chapter 2 for the values of each letter.)

THE MEANING OF EACH HEART'S DESIRE (HD)

HEART'S DESIRE 1

HD 1's are independent, individualistic, born leaders. They want to lead most of all, to take charge and to set the standard for any situation in which they are involved. They are energetic, determined, and ambitious. If they are not in charge, they are restless and discontented. They are often executives or business owners, which provides them with the opportunity to scope out the territory ahead, set the course for the organization, develop innovative approaches to get there, and oversee the entire journey.

When not tempered with consideration for others and tact, HD 1's can be headstrong, overbearing, and impulsive. This can alienate others – and some HD 1's simply pursue solo ventures to avoid dealing with this kind of discomfort. When the HD energy is dormant, the 1 may shirk responsibility or hesitate to step into their natural leadership role, citing self-doubt. When the energy is dominant and healthy, the 1 confidently leads and is about the business of pioneering in the area of their passion.

HEART'S DESIRE 2

HD 2's want harmony most of all and can't tolerate conflict – they want peace and to support others. HD 2's have a genuine concern for others, and love to share with others or help fulfill people's needs. Their first choice is to achieve their desired results harmoniously and through consensus; but if need be they will become assertive. They are emotionally sensitive and are drawn into relationships easily. In fact, they are highly intuitive – with other spiritual gifts and abilities – but may not initially realize this about themselves. They can see both sides of any situation.

Because they depend so much on others, they often mistrust their own inner wisdom. Emotional authenticity – being willing to step up and say what they really feel – is key to obtaining for the HD 2. When the HD energy is dormant, the 2 may become codependent, feeling like they have lost themselves in others. When it is dominant and healthy, the HD 2 is engaged in harmonious relationships with both business colleagues and personal/family ties and feels at peace.

HEART'S DESIRE 3

HD 3's want most of all to make people happy, to create enthusiasm, to encourage and to laugh – they love life! They enjoy parties and social gatherings, great conversation, and entertaining people. If they are not creating, they are unhappy. They need to express their many creative talents – at home and at work – or they will feel stifled. HD 3's often work in a field involving self-expression such as speaking, writing or creative arts.

When not expressing themselves fully, the HD 3 can tend to overcommunicate, isolate, or fantasize. Their energies are easily scattered, since they have a constant stream of new ideas. They need an anchor (such as discipline and hard work) – and often, some assistance with managing their money – so that their platform for expressing themselves creatively is solid. When the HD energy is dormant, the 3 may feel rule-bound or as though they can't vary from the routine (depending on the other numbers in their profile). When the energy is dominant, HD 3's are the happiest and most interesting people of all to be around.

HEART'S DESIRE 4

HD 4's want most to have a plan, to create structure, and to approach things in a practical way – they dislike surprises. They are very dependable and practical, using their strategic thinking ability to see and explain how things fit together (even if they might not seem to at first!). And they long for order, for understanding of how it all works, and for the opportunity to create something lasting. If everything is in chaos, they feel driven to restore order. They want things to be "right" – and value structure over freedom. They can be somewhat serious, and are deeply dedicated to their family.

When not tempered by a healthy attitude of openness, the HD 4 can become rule-bound, obsessive, and compulsive. This can alienate others until they learn the value of compromise, of thinking outside the box, and seeking innovation when it is in the interest of the greater good of the project. When the HD energy is dormant, the 4 may become controlling or cling stubbornly to the way it "should be" – even in the face of change. When it is dominant and healthy, HD 4's establish new order wherever they go, without becoming obsessive – and creates something of lasting value by doing so.

HEART'S DESIRE 5

HD 5's want freedom most of all – from the rules, from restriction, and from feeling trapped. And they love to travel! They may be seen as "Bohemian," since they are enthusiastic, progressive, self-expressive and always changing. They get bored by routine – whether at home or at work. If they are feel confined, they will escape, rebel or otherwise act impulsively. What drives them is the desire for new experiences – a constant stream of them! This can lead to multiple areas of focus and difficulty choosing a career direction or a mate for fear they will miss out on other possibilities.

Until they learn how to balance freedom with structure, the HD 5 can be flighty, superficial, and susceptible to addiction. This can tire friends and family who see the 5 avoiding settling down – or finding an outlet for their talents that allows sufficient variety with security and stability too. When the HD energy is dormant, the 5 may continually shift from one thing to another, unwilling to make a commitment. When it is dominant and healthy, the HD 5 adapts easily to change and has just the right amount of focus and commitment to create a full and financially rewarding life.

HEART'S DESIRE 6

HD 6's want to nurture their home, family, and beauty most – they are true romantics. And they bring this orientation to their work and business too! They are loyal, affectionate, and generous – to the point that sometimes they stifle their own needs for the needs of their friends, family or others in need. They love to share their advice – and are sought out for support and advice by others who value their listening skills. At their core, they wish to love and be loved in return.

Until they set healthy personal boundaries, the HD 6 (like the HD 2) can be codependent, needy, and dependent. This can repel the very relationships that matter most to them, which is often the catalyst for counseling or education to learn how to adequately value the self. When the HD energy is dormant, the 6 may be in relationships but not as invested as they are later. When the energy is dominant and healthy, they will be surrounded with beautiful, mutually satisfying long-term relationships.

HEART'S DESIRE 7

HD 7's want most to have solitude and a good book! They love knowledge, research, analysis – and may also be highly intuitive or spiritual and interested in metaphysical or spiritual subjects. They are very introverted, and require long periods of solitude to study, think and integrate their ideas. Their quest is to find the answers to life's questions – whether that be in the monastery, the research laboratory or the university.

Because of their strong analytical and/or intuitive natures, HD 7's struggle to understand and connect with emotions. In fact, many never marry – and when they do, the couple may spend periods apart to allow the 7 adequate time for reflection. When the HD energy is dormant, 7's isolate, bury themselves in reading or work, and shun interpersonal contact. When the energy is dominant and healthy, the HD 7 balance solitude with interaction, and love sharing what they have concluded from their reflection with those who are interested.

HEART'S DESIRE 8

HD 8's want most to be in charge, to be the boss, and to have power. They are very ambitious, business-focused and intuitively know how to attract and manage money well. They see the big picture vision, and draw others to them to execute the details of the plan. HD 8's want to be respected, to feel important, and to have status. They desire and create wealth, but may find that they have financial challenges – even bankruptcy – on the way to their Heart's Desire.

Until they find the balance between the greater good and the money, power and success that comes naturally to them, they can be so work-focused that they alienate their families. They may also try to "manage" their personal relationships instead of just loving people. When the HD energy is dormant, the 8 may become controlling, manipulative, and authoritative – focused only on the result ("the means justifies the end"). When the energy is dominant and healthy, they will use their natural business and financial acumen to create an empire that does good in the world, while striking the proper balance between work and family.

HEART'S DESIRE 9

HD 9's want most to be of service, make the world a better place, and to love all that's in it. They are philanthropically minded, compassionate and idealistic. Their emotions run deep, and they can become crushed when their idealistic vision fails to materialize. Others look to the HD 9 for inspiration, since they can see what's possible and communicate it to others!

Until they set healthy personal boundaries, the HD 9 can be overgiving and become resentful, feeling they are being taken advantage of. When the HD energy is dormant, the 6 may be involved in day-to-day living but not sense the greater good – or their role in improving it. When the energy is dominant and healthy, they will be surrounded by people who are inspired by them, and will be championing a cause about which they feel passionate.

HEART'S DESIRE 11

HD 11's want most to illuminate the consciousness of others and to bring peace to all of their relationships. They have wisdom beyond their years (since they are often old souls) and are healers, harmonizers, and seek enlightenment above all. They are born with great sensitivity to others' feelings and thoughts – and may also have spiritual healing abilities. This can be disturbing to them as children until they accept their special nature! They will tend to have more emotional ups and downs than other numbers, and may be raised in a turbulent family setting. However, since the 11 also represents the double 1 (leader) energy, they ultimately will become the spiritual leaders they were born to be if their Heart's Desire is fulfilled.

Until they fully accept the calling of their Master number Heart's Desire, the HD 11 can be depressive, feel lost, and feel different from others. When the HD energy is dormant, the 11 may be rejected, aloof, and prone to escapism. When the energy is dominant and healthy, they will be the most inspirational and high-energy people of all to be around, and can transform everyone's life they touch.

HEART'S DESIRE 22

HD 22's want most of all to build something tangible to benefit humanity and outlive the individual. They are big picture thinkers with tremendous intelligence, creativity and sensitivity (from the Master number energy of the 22). Being old souls incarnate, they use their innate desire to build, to create foundation and to establish structure first in mechanical pursuits, and then in global transformation or inventions. The 22 energy requires time to develop, and may emerge in surprising ways along the path of the HD 22's life.

Until they fully accept the calling of their Master number Heart's Desire, the HD-22 may feel awkward, lack confidence, and feel like a misfit. When the HD energy is dormant, the 22 may toil along in engineering, mechanical or other routine careers until the energy awakens within them. When the energy is dominant and healthy, they will be about the business of changing the world in some unique and global way, through their ideas and inventions (and spiritual insights).

No matter what your Heart's Desire number is, know that it holds the key to your ultimate fulfillment and satisfaction in life. Remembering its inner motivation will help you better understand the best outer Expression of the gifts that lie within you.

15

BIRTHDAY NUMBER –
WHAT IT ADDS TO YOUR
INSPIRED SUCCESS PATH

Numerologists believe that your soul chose your birthday because that day reflected what you need in this life to help you fulfill your Inspired Success Path. Often, it adds missing energetic traits to the Core Profile that are essential for the whole person.

In my own case, my Life Path is 1, Expression 4 and Heart's Desire 4 – which is a lot of intense, hard-working energy! Being born on the 20th gives me the softening effect of the 2 – peacemaker and harmonizer, along with the 0, which provides intuitive insights to assist my strong intellectual capacity. I am grateful for the blend of both whenever I am in the midst of one or more projects!

HOW TO COMPUTE YOUR BIRTHDAY NUMBER

To compute your Birthday Number, simply take the day itself (not month or year) for your birthday number – then look at the summary of that birthday number below to see what it means for you. Example: if you were born March 15, 1965, your Birthday Number is 15.

If you were born on a double digit day (10 or higher) it is used both as the double digit and its single digit sum, so look at the meaning of both numbers to determine the full meaning for you. To reduce it to the lowest common denominator, you add the two digits (1 + 0 = 1). If you were born on the 11th or 22nd, these are Master Numbers and have special meaning (see below).

(Also think of your family or staff members' birthdays as you review the following list and see if their birthday characterizes them.)

MEANING OF EACH BIRTHDAY NUMBER

1 – You were born to be first, a leader (leading the month)! Individuality is key for you, and you are highly independent. You easily become frustrated with routine. Innovation is natural for the 1 birthday. You are able to motivate others and have a great vision. (Ron Howard is a 1)

2 – You seek balance and harmony, and are a natural mediator. You are a natural peacemaker. Sensitive, intuitive and diplomatic, you love beauty and attention. You work best in partnerships or as being the power behind the throne, rather than the king himself. (Mikhail Gorbachev was a 2)

3 – This is seen as a lucky birthday and indicates blessings! You have a highly developed creative talent, are highly imaginative, and have great enthusiasm. Your sense of fun and friendliness is contagious. You have a childlike, happy spirit. (Martha Stewart is a 3)

4 – A 4 birthday indicates you appreciate both form and order. You are a hard worker and a conscientious person, precise and take great care at what you do. You are highly principled, disciplined and responsible – and you take your obligations seriously! Your strengths are the slow, patient approach, and being methodical. (Feminist Betty Friedan was a 4)

5 – The 5 birthday usually means risk-taking comes naturally. Quick and clever, 5's embrace change, travel and adventure. They are highly adaptable, and need excitement. They have trouble being bound to a desk or office, and become bored easily. Beware of impulsiveness and addiction though! (Hank Aaron was a 5)

6 – If you have a 6 birthday, you are emotional, sensitive, and love deeply and seriously. Family is very important to you, and you have a talent for settling disputes between people. Balance is a key life lesson for the 6. They need to know they are appreciated and will sacrifice their own comfort to help others. (George W. Bush is a 6)

7 – The 7 birthday indicates a highly developed mind and great analytical ability. Sevens also have excellent intuition. They may appear aloof to others, but this is simply a reflection of their need for solitude. They prefer to work alone, and can be opinionated and stubborn. (Katie Couric is a 7)

8 – The 8 birthday brings a talent for business and a good sense of money. Characterized by strength of character, good judgment and a solid value system, 8's can handle large projects with ease. They are ambitious and have a strong desire for material success and security – so like being in charge. (Harry S Truman was an 8)

9 – The 9 birthday embodies the humanitarian impulse. They are broad-minded, idealistic and compassionate. Artistic and philanthropic, it is important that 9's be involved in a career that serves the greater good. You may take your time before choosing a profession. Nines attract money from unexpected sources. (John Lennon was a 9)

10 – The 10 birthday brings in the leadership of the 1 (1 + 0 = 1) and is ambitious, original, determined and enterprising. They love start-up projects that draw on their independence and courageous nature. They are frustrated by routine and can be stubborn and rigid on occasion. (Osama bin Laden was a 10)

11 – The 11 birthday is a master level of the 2 energy (1 + 1 = 2) and indicates a highly intuitive, high-energy person. Idealism, inspiration, and innovation characterize the 11. You excel in determination but do not do well in business (except as an adviser). Your life is an example for others. (Steve Wozniak of Apple is an 11)

12 – The 12 birthday indicates someone who is friendly, enthusiastic, and individualistic. Similar to the 3 (1 + 2 = 3), creativity and communication come naturally. You can be the life of the party and have a fun, friendly nature that draws others to you. (Ozzy Osbourne is a 12)

13 – The 13 birthday brings a twist on the 4 energy (1 + 3 = 4) in that the 1 leadership and the 3 creativity and communication merge here. 13's are creative, energetic, self-disciplined and practical. You may have health problems, and/or be challenged to work hard and apply yourself despite limitations. (John Nash "beautiful mind" was a 13)

14 – The 14 birthday loves change, excitement and travel. 14's embody calculated risk taking, and involve lessons in the correct use of responsibility. 14's can be erratic when they shirk responsibility, but will be challenged with frequent changes, travel opportunities and chances to adapt to the new. (Albert Einstein was a 14 as is Donald Trump)

15 – A combination of the 1 and 5 energy, the 15 is responsible but independent at the same time. They are highly creative and artistic, and have a yearning to become grounded within a family or community structure. Commitment to relationships is a theme in their lives. (Ben Affleck is a 15)

16 – The 16 birthday blends leadership and family in an interesting way: they may find their life brings sudden (or dramatic) events that require you to look at your life more honestly. 16's need time to rest, meditate and contemplate, and may have unusual interest in scientific or spiritual/metaphysical topics. (John McEnroe and Madonna are both 16's)

17 – The 17 birthday brings capable success in the business world. Taking an original approach, you are ambitious if not self-centered. A natural leader, you are best suited to a management role in a company or leadership of your own enterprise. (Robert de Niro is a 17)

18 – The 18 birthday is broadminded with a humanitarian focus. They can work well with others but must preserve their independence. They tend to inspire others and have excellent potential for financial success and achievement. They can be dramatic at times. (Paul McCartney is an 18)

19 – The 19 birthday embodies determination and longs for independence. They may be tested to respond compassionately and to contribute to the betterment of others due to the karmic nature of this birthday. Their challenge is to discern the dream of independence versus its reality. (Bill Clinton and Ted Turner are both 19's)

20 – The 20 birthday indicates compassion, cooperation and adaptability. The 0 in the day suggests a strong intuition too. 20's can sense others' feelings even when they try to hide them. They are moved by beauty, harmony and love. They are excellent advisors to those in power. (Buzz Aldrin and Nicole Kidman are 20's)

21 – Those with a 21 birthday see being social as second nature. They are creative, imaginative, inspiring and enthusiastic. They excel at sales. Their challenge is to focus on one profession versus scattering their energies. (Placido Domingo and Goldie Hawn are 21's)

22 – The 22 birthday is a Master number, the 22/4, or Master Builder. They have great potential as a leader, organizer, or builder of an enterprise – and have the vision and capability to make it happen. They must use their intuition and practical solutions to manifest things that benefit humankind. (George Washington was a 22)

23 – The 23 birthday embodies the 5 energy by blending cooperation with creativity and communicative talents. 23's are emotionally sensitive, creative and intuitive, and are gifted quick thinkers. They welcome change and excitement in their life. (Leonardo da Vinci and Bruce Springstein are 23's)

24 – The 24 birthday brings the combined talents of mediation/cooperation and hard work to this person's life. They are determined (even stubborn) and place great focus on their home and family. They are excellent at continuing an enterprise someone else has started. They have a gift for the healing and cultural arts. (Steve Jobs was a 24)

25 – The 25 birthday possesses a sound, rational mind and keen insight. 25's can bring unique or unusual approaches to solutions. They have a good intuition, are sensitive, and reflect on themselves and the meaning of life. They may be drawn to spiritual or psychic exploration. (Christopher Reeve was a 25)

26 – The 26 birthday has a good sense of money and a talent for business. They are practical and responsible yet feel strongly about people – especially their family. Their lesson is to be a source of strength to others without having to be in charge. (Hillary Clinton is a 26)

27 – The 27 birthday represents someone who is both analytical and intuitive – with a humanitarian bent. They may appear detached or withdrawn to others, since they like to keep their true feelings to themselves. There is an element of sacrifice here, as well as concern for the planet. (Henry Kissinger was a 27)

28– The 28 birthday has a gift for leadership, but it is best used through cooperation with others. Characterized by determination and independence, 28's may feel like they are fighting themselves when they need to follow the rules – but they bounce back from any setbacks. (Alan Alda and Bill Gates are 28's)

29 – The 29 birthday brings personality and great potential (2 + 9 = 11, a master number). They are intuitive, illuminators, and dreamers – so may be moody. They seek inner peace. They love beauty and harmony and have leadership abilities. (John F. Kennedy and Oprah Winfrey are 29's)

30 – The 30 birthday embodies the creativity and communication talents of the 3, but with the intuition indicated by the 0. This gives you tremendous power with words and the ability to inspire others. Friendly, imaginative and sociable, 30's have a good sense of harmony and art in all they do. (Truman Capote, Eric Clapton and Tiger Woods are 30's)

31 – The 31 birthday brings a great love of family, tradition and community. 31's work hard, are strong-willed and determined but also have original ideas that they systematically implement. They are practical and grounded, building a strong foundation for the future. Discipline characterizes the 31 – which can become rigidity if not balanced. (J.K. Rowling is a 31)

Now that you know your Birthday Number, consider what its energy adds to the three Core Numbers we explored previously (Life Path, Expression and Heart's Desire) as they relate to your business or profession. Does your work allow you to express your natural gifts as much as you would like? Are you appreciated and acknowledged for it? And if not, what other fields of endeavor call to you that would be a better fit?

16

PERSONALITY NUMBER - HOW OTHERS SEE YOU

As Julie (whom we met in chapter 8) was developing the plan to open her coaching and speaking business to help parents of troubled teens support their children during tough times, she found that people were already seeking her out before she opened the doors. They were drawn to her effusive personality, wit, and charm – as well as her past experiences with her own teenage son. As she went about her commitments in the community and the word got out, local groups were asking her to speak to them about what she had learned even before she was officially in business.

Why did people find Julie so magnetic and put their confidence in her at such an early stage? It was due to her Personality Number 3. They saw her as a confident, creative communicator with a bubbly personality, and knew without her convincing them that she would persuasively share her knowledge when she coached or spoke to them.

WHAT IS THE PERSONALITY NUMBER?

The *Personality number* is *what you project to others before they get to know you on a deeper basis. It is your outer shell, or how others perceive you.* Whether they meet you in a networking meeting or other setting, see you online, hear you speak, or see a photograph of you, your Personality Number is your "calling card" and first impression.

If you don't know what vibration they are sensing, you will automatically assume they can see the true, inner you. But the Personality Number serves as a doorway or entrance to that inner you – and it usually provides a much smaller concept of who you are so that it is safe to share this with strangers or first-time acquaintances. Does it invite them in to know more (as Julie's does above), or does it cause them to be suspicious or uninterested to know more?

The Personality Number is derived from adding the energetic vibration of each of the consonants in your name. (Refer to the chart in chapter 2 for the value of each letter.)

THE MEANING OF EACH PERSONALITY NUMBER (PN)

PERSONALITY NUMBER 1

PN 1's are seen as dominant, forceful, confident, independent, courageous, and professional. They radiate energy, appear confident, and tend to dress in bright colors. They convey confidence and the willingness to take risks, and are recognized as pioneers who will take the initiative to get something new started. When running their own business or a large organization, people feel confident putting their trust in the PN 1. They instinctively know the 1 will do what is necessary to take the lead and ensure the desired result is reached.

If 1's are not feeling balanced, they may come across as lacking confidence or, alternately, overbearing and obnoxious.

PERSONALITY NUMBER 2

PN 2's are seen as friendly, charming, reserved, shy, clean and neat. They dislike the limelight and conflict – and can be people-pleasing. They desire harmony and compatible relationships. Their sensitivity (emotionally or spiritually) may also be evident in a first-time meeting. They may seem compliant in the face of differing viewpoints, since they dislike conflict. They are able to see both sides of any situation. When they are happily involved in compatible relationships, they blossom and people seek them out.

If 2's are not feeling balanced, they may become codependent, feeling like they have lost themselves in others.

PERSONALITY NUMBER 3

PN 3's are seen as entertaining, charming, extroverted, attractive, optimistic, enthusiastic, friendly, charismatic, animate, fun and charismatic. They love to make people happy, to create enthusiasm, to encourage and to laugh – they love life! If they are not creating or spending time with others, they will be unhappy.

If 3's are not feeling balanced, they may come across as scattered, flippant or exaggerating, and their conversation can become superficial.

PERSONALITY NUMBER 4

PN 4's are seen as conservative, shy, reserved, honest, compliant, hardworking, and practical. They reassure others through their ability to see how things fit together, and to build a solid foundation and effective systems to do anything. They long for order, for understanding of how it all works, and for the opportunity to create something lasting. They want things to be "right" – and value structure over freedom. They can be somewhat serious, and are deeply dedicated to their family.

If 4's are not feeling balanced, they may come across as rule-bound, obsessive, and compulsive. This can alienate others until they learn the value of compromise, of thinking outside the box, and seeking innovation when it is in the interest of the greater good of the project.

PERSONALITY NUMBER 5

PN 5's are seen as magnetic, sexually appealing, witty, outgoing, youthful looking, sensual, and adaptable. They are exciting to be with because they constantly seek freedom and new experiences. They get bored by routine – whether at home or at work. They are interesting conversationalists because of their multiple areas of interest.

If 5's are not feeling balanced, they may come across as flighty, superficial, and susceptible to addiction.

PERSONALITY NUMBER 6

PN 6's are seen as nurturers, protectors, loyal idealists, great problem-solvers, gracious, good hosts, and domestic. They dress in comfortable clothes, and make people feel comfortable in their presence. Their priority is their family, and they will often carry family photos with them. They are true romantics! And they bring this orientation to their work and business too.

If 6's are not feeling balanced, they may come across as codependent, needy, and dependent. This can repel the very relationships that matter most to them, which is often the catalyst for counseling or education to learn how to adequately value the self.

PERSONALITY NUMBER 7

PN 7's are seen as aloof, loners, studious, mystical, introspective, introverted, intelligent, mysterious, and eccentric. They love knowledge, research, analysis – and may also be highly intuitive or spiritual and interested in metaphysical or spiritual subjects. They are very introverted, and require long periods of solitude to study, think and integrate their ideas. Therefore, they can be somewhat unapproachable or shy, but enjoy discussing their topics of study once they build initial rapport with someone.

If 7's are not feeling balanced, they may come across as aloof, loners and uncaring, since 7's struggle to understand and connect with emotions. In fact, many never marry – and when they do, the couple may spend periods apart to allow the 7 adequate time for reflection.

PERSONALITY NUMBER 8

PN 8's are seen as authoritative, power-conscious, in control, strong, visionary, organized, assertive, dresses for success, and business-minded. They love being in charge, being the boss, and having power – and are alternately viewed as highly successful or snobbish and bossy. They are very ambitious, business-focused and intuitively know how to attract and manage money well. PN-8's want to be respected, to feel important, and to have status.

If 8's are not feeling balanced, they may come across as so work-focused that they alienate their families. They may also try to "manage" their personal relationships instead of just loving people.

PERSONALITY NUMBER 9

PN 9's are seen as idealistic, cares about others, emotional, intuitive, indecisive, abstract, sympathetic, generous, and philosophical. They are service-oriented, and others sense their desire to make the world a better place. They are philanthropically minded, compassionate and idealistic. Their emotions run deep, and they can become crushed when their idealistic vision fails to materialize. Others look to the PN 9 for inspiration, since they can see what's possible and communicate it to others!

If 9's are not feeling balanced, they may come across as overgiving and resentful, feeling they are being taken advantage of.

$$6\ 8\ 4$$
$$2\ \mathbf{1}\ 5\ 7$$
$$9\ \mathbf{1}\ 3\ 7$$
$$0\ 3$$

17

MATURITY NUMBER – HOW YOUR BUSINESS/CAREER FOCUS CHANGES LATER IN LIFE

After selling her real estate firm, Susan (whom we met in chapter 10) entered a time of personal crisis. She felt uncertain what to do next – or even who she wanted to be next. She had all the money she wanted from the $10 million sale...but something was missing. Susan explored many options, and ultimately decided to go back to school to get her master's degree in transformational psychology. She increasingly felt drawn to both deepen her knowledge and to explore how people successfully changed – their behavior, their beliefs, and their lives (particularly following tragedies and setbacks). Though this seemed a huge departure from finance, business and real estate, it felt absolutely right to her in her 40's to be moving in this new direction.

What Susan experienced was the emergence of her Maturity Number – which was the energy of the number 7, focusing on deep study, research and analysis as well as spiritual or metaphysical topics. This energy, as we will see below, can be palpable in childhood but then go dormant until sometime between the ages of 35 and 45, when it emerges as a dominant theme in the chart and the person's life again.

WHAT IS THE MATURITY NUMBER?

The fifth and last of the Core Numbers is your *Maturity number*, which is *your underlying goal, wish or desire that emerges as you better understand yourself and your intended life outcomes*. If you are over the age of 35, this is the dominant energy of your experience for the rest of your life. It normally doesn't arise until at least age 35 – sometimes as late as age 50 – but becomes a core focus for you. And you usually experience a shift in your life when it does!

The Maturity Number is derived by combining the energies of your Life Path and your Expression number, so it is known as the "nature of your true self" or the "ultimate goal" of your life. It is your highest vibration. Of course, as we grow we come to realize more of who we are, what we really want, and what is important in life. That is reflected in the Maturity Number – and its influence increases with age.

When we are younger, we may have a vague awareness of this energy, but it is usually not consciously felt until midlife. However, it is nevertheless present and affects many of our decisions and actions from the subconscious realm – especially at key moments and turning points in life. Your Maturity Number energy is what you have mastered when you are at your peak of development. Dr. Juno Jordan calls it the "lighthouse at the end of the road" of your life.

THE MEANING OF EACH MATURITY NUMBER (MN)

Following is the interpretation of each Maturity Number:

MATURITY NUMBER 1

Those with a MN 1 will feel a need for increasing independence and leadership in the second half of their life. Drawing on the lessons learned about this topic in early childhood, they will find themselves in leadership roles – but need to be careful not to be overbearing or bossy when they lead. The MN 1 can be "set in their ways" – usually around one specific topic in their life.

Starting a business in midlife is a natural for people with an MN 1, since it lets them express their leadership in the way they see fit. Failing to either have their own business or a leadership role in a company will leave them frustrated.

MATURITY NUMBER 2

Those with a MN 2 can expect to find others willing to help them and will naturally attract support in the second half of their life. Drawing on the lessons learned about this topic in early childhood, they now know that giving first leads to receiving most, and helpfulness is key. Their sensitivity to others can be uncanny, having been honed over years. They become excellent persuaders and peacemakers and are likely to pursue artistic endeavors in the latter half of life.

Being in relationship – and in business, partnership – is something the MN 2 seeks. And helping others find peace, harmony and cooperation through their work is an ideal fit.

MATURITY NUMBER 3

Those with a MN 3 will find themselves expressing artistic talent and creative imagination in the second half of their life. Drawing on the lessons learned about this topic in early childhood, they will direct their verbal and written communication abilities toward creative projects. They will notice a zest, enthusiasm and joy for life.

People with a MN 3 do very well financially when working in harmony with their world and expressing their creative gifts through art or speaking or other communication vehicle.

MATURITY NUMBER 4

Those with a MN 4 will find themselves making the dreams they have had practical, using discipline and hard work in the second half of their life. Drawing on the lessons learned about this topic in early childhood, they will be more practical, organized and down to earth than they were earlier in life. They will create opportunities to contribute to something lasting. It is important for these people to avoid becoming rigid or self-righteous, but they will naturally hold to their principles in all they do.

The MN 4 will be devoted to the business or work which they have chosen. No quiet retirement here! Working on a project that is lasting through their work is the ideal fit for the 4.

MATURITY NUMBER 5

Those with a MN 5 will find themselves living an exciting, full life in midlife and beyond! Frequent change, travel, and true independence (balancing responsibility with freedom) characterizes the MN 5. Drawing on the lessons learned about this topic in early childhood, they continue to learn from their own experiences but also know to gain all they can from each experience before moving on.

In business, the MN 5 makes a great leader because they seek progressive, fun and exciting approaches. They may continue to struggle to find stability and commitment in later life, but are seen as "forever young."

MATURITY NUMBER 6

Those with a MN 6 will find the welfare and well-being of others to be paramount in the second half of their life. Their concern broadens beyond their family to the human family at large, and a humanitarian focus is common. Drawing on the lessons learned about this topic in early childhood, the surround themselves with beauty and with people who love being in their presence. They are truly happy when helping the world in some way.

In business, roles as a healer, counselor, teacher or similar role allow the MN 6 to nurture and care for others through their work.

MATURITY NUMBER 7

Those with a MN 7 will be quite comfortable charting their own course and requiring solitude for reflection and analysis in the second half of their life. Left to their own devices, they will find an area in which to truly shine in their later life. Drawing on the lessons learned about this topic in early childhood, they continue to value finding the truth – in whatever form – and even when excited by their discoveries others may seem them as aloof. MN 7's enjoy the finer things in life.

MN 7's may become known for an invention or innovation that results from their hours of solitude. It is important that they follow their intuition on the way to those discoveries.

MATURITY NUMBER 8

Those with a MN 8 will reap rewards through business, finance and accomplishment in the second half of their life. Work may become more important to them, though they struggle to balance material and spiritual (the loops of the 8) in pursuing their purpose. Drawing on the lessons learned about this topic in early childhood, they are willing to work hard, to direct, to organize, and may experience ups and downs financially in their latter life.

In business, MN 8's are natural leaders – all the way to the end of their life. They need to be mindful that their natural self-reliance can make them seem unapproachable to others. It is also important to focus on the greater good – not just material success – to fulfill the calling of the MN 8.

MATURITY NUMBER 9

Those with a MN 9 will find that life carries challenges with it, for they are called to make personal sacrifices for the sake of the spiritual or greater good in the second half of their life. Things will come easily to the 9, but their gifts are meant to be used to better humanity, not for personal gain. Drawing on the lessons learned about this topic in early childhood, they exercise their compassion and humanitarian interests in a healthy (not codependent) way. Their greatest good is through giving.

In business, serving humanity in some way is key in midlife and beyond. Involvement in the arts, performing, writing, teaching or philanthropy are a perfect fit.

MATURITY NUMBER 11

Those with a MN 11 have a Master Maturity Number and will find their intuition, psychic abilities and self-understanding increase with the years. Drawing on their childhood awareness and experiences, they need to learn to temper their highly charged nature with excellent diet, rest, exercise and self-care. Others may at times find these people too intense – but the challenge is not to let that discourage the MN 11 from expressing him/herself, but to discern how much of their power a given person can master.

MATURITY NUMBER 22

Those with a MN 22 have a Master Maturity Number and will find an increased ability to make things happen, as the Master Builder, in the second half of their life. Their childhood may be challenging, but in maturity their management and leadership ability emerges. Many tests and challenges will come the way of the MN 22. They always need to have a goal or a mission through which to channel the 22/4 energy.

BRINGING IT ALL TOGETHER

Can you see now how the numbers within your profile tell a story about your life and work direction and purpose? Here's a recap of what we've explored so far:

- Numerology is the *study of the energy of numbers, as revealed in the birth date and birth name of a person*

- Your Inspired Success Path is a combination of your *Life Path number (the natural talents and abilities that you brought to this lifetime, that you can do without training) and your Expression number (the area you sought to master, and through which you desire to express yourself, in this lifetime).*

- Your *Inspired Success Path* gives you your soul's agenda for the type of industry, work or business that is right for you, and your role within that context

- Your *Heart's Desire Number* provides your inner motivation and is your inner yearning, or what you wish to accomplish through your work and life

- Your *Personality Number* is how others see you before they know you well

- And your *Maturity Number,* your underlying goal, wish or desire that emerges as you better understand yourself and your intended life outcomes is an energy that emerges in childhood and then becomes dormant until midlife when it re-emerges around age 35-45 and increases in intensity throughout the rest of your life

Now we will examine three common barriers to success that you will want to know how to overcome to fully express your Inspired Success Path and to align your business or career with your soul's agenda.

PART FOUR:

COMMON BARRIERS TO SUCCESS

In this Part, we will explore three common causes of barriers or blockage to the full expression of your Inspired Success Path – and how to overcome them - including:

- Karmic Debt and Karmic Lessons

- Energy Blocks in Your Chakras

- Sabotaging or Outdated Beliefs

18

CONFRONTING KARMA IN YOUR NAME OR PROFILE

After a normal middle-class upbringing, Jenny got her degree in psychology and went to work in a university career center helping graduates get jobs. Even though the college was somewhat lax in its structures, as an Inspired Success Path 4-11 Jenny brought both organization and harmony to the way she served the students. When she was 29, Jenny was headed home for spring break when the car she was riding in was hit by an 18-wheel trailer/tractor, and she was seriously wounded by her injuries. In fact, when she woke from her coma she found she had a new skill: she could see auras around people. Jenny was unsure what to think about this, but recognized that it was a special gift. (What she didn't know was that with her 11/2 Expression, this was the emergence of her 11 Spiritual Messenger energy.)

Jenny left the college and searched to find a position that fulfilled her after the accident. She would try new leadership roles and find she either tried to move forward too fast or she shied away from leadership for fear of rejection. It was difficult for her to ask for help

– even when she struggled severely in her work and personal life. For years she wondered what she was really here to do. Finally, as she entered her 40's, she realized that her life's work was to share her aura-reading gifts through readings, healing sessions, and group workshops. She felt wonderful when she was doing the workshops. But the actual preparation and marketing did not come easily, and she frequently doubted herself.

The reason Jenny struggled in the unique way she did is due to karma, the first of three types of blocks we will explore that can keep the Inspired Success Path from being fully expressed. Both her Heart's Desire and Personality Numbers were the 19/1, which as we will learn below brings lessons about standing up for oneself, independence and proper use of power. So even though she had innate leadership ability, the karma prevented her from stepping easily and fully into it and taking charge of her area of responsibility and contribution.

WHAT IS KARMA

Karma is the cosmic principle which says that *each person is rewarded or punished in one lifetime according to that person's deeds in a previous lifetime.* It recognizes that "what goes around comes around," and "we reap what we sow." The exact nature of the payback that will occur depends on the specific number in the person's profile. Karma can appear either as Karmic Debt or as Karmic Lessons.

KARMIC DEBT NUMBERS

There are four numbers representing *"Karmic Debts"* in numerology: 13, 14, 16, and 19. And each of them has a different focus. They are "debts" in the sense that *something occurred in the past lifetime in which the person acquired power, love, freedom or a similar outcome at the expense of another (or more than one person).* No debt goes unpaid! So it is part of that person's life agenda this time to repay that debt by avoiding similar selfish abuses and acting for the good of both themselves and others. Karmic Debt numbers have particular significance when they are found in the core numbers: Life Path, Expression, Heart's Desire, Personality or Maturity Number – or Birthday.

When it comes to business, Karmic Debts in one's core numbers can make the Inspired Success Path the person – or the business – is on a bit bumpy, and they will have additional burdens and/or a harder time making progress than someone who has no Karmic Debt in their profile. As a result, they will be held to a higher standard. Since you have control over when you found a business and what you name it, you can avoid karma in its name and life path – and I recommend you do!

Karmic Debts are expressed with the 2-digit number first, a slash, and the single digit total, e.g., 13/4. This indicates that while the 4 energy is present, it is a karmic 4.

The good news is that once the debt is overcome or "paid back," the karmic influence dissipates – it does not need to last an entire lifetime.

THE MEANING OF EACH KARMIC DEBT

KARMIC DEBT 13/4

The 13/4 in someone's profile denotes a debt related to hard work. In a past lifetime, they likely avoided hard work or discipline or were prone to laziness. They allowed others to carry their share of the burden and wanted the easy way out. Therefore, in this lifetime they will have to work harder than others do to obtain the same result. Frustration and feelings of futility can definitely result! 13/4's will be unlikely to have easy "breaks" in life.

The key lesson for 13/4's is to focus their energy, keep their commitments, and apply discipline and hard work to their life. In addition, 13/4's are learning to bring spiritual consciousness into their work and other ways of expressing themselves. They must maintain order and make a steady and constant effort, and avoid temptations to once again take the easy or softer way. When they begin to feel like "it isn't worth it" or "it's too much work," that's the Karmic Debt rearing its ugly head again. That's what got them into trouble the last time around, so they need to keep plugging away until they reach the desired result.

At some point on their journey – as they are learning the lessons that accompany this Karmic Debt – they will likely display the negative aspect of the 4 energy, such as rigidity, black-and-white thinking, being rule-bound, being controlling, and even blaming others for their perceived limitations.

Business applications: 13/4's will need to choose a profession or area of focus and stay with it for the long-term, building solid foundations and making steady progress in building their business (or progressing in their career). Trying to find shortcuts or bypassing required steps will backfire on them (and could create more karma). They will need to establish systems for their life and work that allow them to stay organized, keep a schedule, stay current on financial obligations, and complete commitments they make.

KARMIC DEBT 14/5

The 14/5 in someone's profile denotes a debt related to abuse of freedom. They may have misused, avoided or misunderstood freedom in a past life. Perhaps they gained their freedom at the expense of another, resulting in a lack of accountability and responsibility for their actions. Their life will seem like a roller coaster, with frequent (and often unanticipated) changes to which they will need to learn to adapt.

The key lesson for 14/5's is to bring freedom into balance in this lifetime. They need to embrace commitment – in relationships and work – and bring order to their lives to counteract the internal quest for freedom.

At some point on their journey – as they are learning the lessons that accompany this Karmic Debt – they will likely display the negative aspect of the 5 energy, such as addiction or other forms of escape, job hopping, frequent relationship changes, and refusing to accept responsibility. Ultimately, they learn that by persevering with something is a more constructive path to freedom.

Business applications: 14/5's may go through an initial period of job hopping and trying on different college majors and/or careers before they settle down. Their success will be found when they discover a career path or business that contains enough variety and change to keep them stimulated while still staying in the same organization or industry. They may leverage their well-honed ability to manage change by helping companies with change management, market shifts, or financial ups and downs.

KARMIC DEBT 16/7

The 16/7 in someone's profile denotes a debt related to abuse of love. They may have acted irresponsibly with regard to matters of love in a past lifetime, having an affair, acting irresponsibly or otherwise causing others to suffer in the area of relationships. As a result, their current lifetime will be filled with challenges of ego destruction and rebirth, as the human self and the inspired self battle for control. They may lose everything and have to start over more than once in an effort to become humble and reliant on God or a Higher Power. The good news is, the rebirth brings entirely new energy and enthusiasm into the 16/7's life, and the struggle seems like it was worth it!

The key lesson for 16/7's is faith. As they navigate the destruction and rebirth cycle that accompanies their karma, they will learn to depend upon a spiritual Source on which to depend as they rebuild each time. Humility and acceptance are the gateway to learning these lessons.

At some point on their journey – as they are learning the lessons that accompany this Karmic Debt – they will likely display the negative aspect of the 7 energy, such as aloofness, indifference, overanalyzing, and withdrawing. During their life, they must learn to be humble, to love and to finally come to a sense of peace which only comes through faith. Eventually, they learn to surrender to the Inspired Will for them and their life begins to flow more smoothly.

Business applications: 16/7's may find their success path interrupted more than once with severe downturns, such as bankruptcy or embezzlement resulting in closing or losing their job or business. Divorce or a health crisis may leave them financially insolvent, requiring that they rebuild or find a new direction that will serve them during the next phase of their life. They can also become stuck if they focus too much on studying, preparing, and getting ready for success – versus taking action to create it.

KARMIC DEBT 19/1

The 19/1 in someone's profile denotes a debt related to power. They may have acted in their own self-interest and abused power in a past lifetime by being overbearing, authoritarian or manipulative. This person not only had power in a past life, but they knew right from wrong – and acted recklessly despite that knowledge. As a result, they hurt others because of their selfish decisions and pursuit of personal desires. In this lifetime, they may find themselves having to stand up for themselves by confronting controlling or abusive parents or bosses, and/or being emotionally authentic in their close relationships even when what they need to share may be received with anger or defensiveness. Their life circumstances may leave them alone – by divorce, job layoff or move – again calling to them to stand up for their own self-interests and get their needs met.

The key lesson for 19/1's is the proper, balanced use of power and independence – as well as how to stand up for themselves.

At some point on their journey – as they are learning the lessons that accompany this Karmic Debt – they will likely display the negative aspect of the 1 energy, such as dependence, failing to stand up for themselves, selfishness, intimidation, resisting help from others, narcissism, laziness, and aggression. During their life, they learn to become independent yet identify with the feelings of others, learn to accept help, and avoid abuse of power. They understand their connectedness with all others and that their actions affect others in a direct way – so they act authentically and with integrity.

Business applications: 19/1's may find themselves shirking leadership or, alternatively, becoming authoritarian leaders (taking a "my way or the highway" approach). Though they have innate leadership tendencies and abilities, they need to learn to lead in an authentic, balanced way that honors and respects others' needs and goals as well as their own. This is particularly called for in the emerging Feminine Leadership Model where dictatorial management is no longer tolerated by many employees.

THE UNIQUE VIBRATION OF THE NUMBER 10

The number 10 is known as the "Wheel of Fortune" in numerology. So if you have a 1 in your profile that was derived from the number 10 (1 + 0 = 1), it represents a special energy! The 10 indicates stands for karmic completion, and means that past Karmic Debts have been paid and the person is entering this lifetime with a "clean slate." All of the positive traits of the 1 through 9 energies are available to you – and you have the opportunity to set new direction for the next phase of your evolution. What do you choose to create?

KARMIC LESSONS IN YOUR NAME

In addition to Karmic Debts, there are Karmic Lessons reflected in which letters are missing in someone's name, and the numerology vibration of that letter. *Karmic Lessons are weaknesses we must work on in this lifetime, or areas which we have not yet had an opportunity to focus or master previously* – so they provide opportunities for growth.

The most common Karmic Lessons are missing 7's and 8's; the most rare Karmic Lesson is a missing 9.

Karmic lesson 1 – invites you to you exercise more initiative, become more determined and strengthen your will. Make your own decisions, stand on your own two feet, and develop more self-confidence.

Karmic lesson 2 – invites you to you be more diplomatic and tactful; stay behind the scenes when need be; and not depend so much on overt praise in order to accomplish something.

Karmic lesson 3 – invites you to you lighten up on yourself, become less critical, and trust your innate abilities.

Karmic lesson 4 – invites you to you find clarity about your life direction and the approach you take to achieving your goals; be more orderly, methodical and disciplined and create a foundation about your life that lasts.

Karmic lesson 5 – invites you to you be more adaptable, adventurous and change-hardy. Overcome the fear of living and take opportunities to fully experience life.

Karmic lesson 6 – invites you to you establish sincere relationships by dropping your guard, making a commitment to marriage or another important relationship, and show true emotion.

Karmic lesson 7 – invites you to you deepen your knowledge and talents in a specific area that appeals to you; be your own critic but don't condemn yourself.

Karmic lesson 8 – invites you to you work at learning how to handle money, be open to the wise opinions of experts that can guide you, and be efficient in managing your resources.

Karmic lesson 9 – invites you to you be more compassionate, understanding and tolerant, and identify with others' trials and tribulations. Broaden your view of life and see things from a larger perspective.

Again, the good news about karma is that it can be overcome and discharged! So be aware of the karmic numbers in your profile, and set about to consciously take actions that will discharge the debt or learn the lesson.

684
2 1 57
9 3 7
0 3

19

DISSOLVING ENERGY BLOCKS TO THE EXPRESSION OF OUR INSPIRED SUCCESS PATH

David, an Inspired Success Path 7-3, had chosen a career in aeronautical engineering and was very successful as an analyst and researcher there. He had pioneered technology that allowed satellites to connect to emergency response systems so that crimes could be solved more quickly. However, when he was asked to present the results of his research to his work team, he froze. He would do anything to avoid these situations, including calling in sick, missing the meetings, or losing his notes. He was terrified – and didn't know why!

David has fallen prey to the second type of common block to the full expression of one's Inspired Success Path: energy blocks in one or more chakras. When he was in first grade, his teacher and classmates ridiculed him because he stuttered, and even as an adult the energy stuck in his throat chakra kept him from being able to present his ideas in public.

THE 7 CHAKRAS

Humans have a magnificent energy system within them known as the seven "chakras." Chakra literally means "wheel" – and each of the seven wheels of energy represent particular qualities in one's life. When a business owner or professional feels stuck – whether money isn't flowing, ideas

aren't coming, or your close relationship(s) are suffering – it is common to find one or more chakras blocked. And each chakra is connected to certain specific aspects of business.

Blockages often arise when we have an experience that is upsetting, tragic, or painful, and we don't fully deal with it at the time. For example, if a business partner let and took a large share of the firm's clients, it would be financially damaging and the remaining partner could feel betrayed, hurt, and afraid. He might store the unresolved energy in his heart chakra to prevent being similarly hurt by someone else – but the blockage also serves as a shield to prevent him from receiving support and love from others in his life.

CHAKRAS AND BUSINESS AREAS AFFECTED

Chakra 1: Root – The root chakra is concerned with our survival and our feeling of belonging on the planet – and to our family or other tribal group. Blockages in this chakra may materialize in the body as low back pain, sciatica, depression and various immune disorders. Stuck first chakra energy affects our ability to launch a business, to get our basic financial needs met, to feel a sense of belonging within our industry, staff and colleagues, and to form a true community among our client or customer base.

Chakra 2: Sacral – The sacral chakra is concerned with creative expression, money and finances, and sexuality. Blockages in this chakra may materialize in the body as low to mid back pain, gynecological or other reproductive organ issues, urinary issues, and the like. Stuck second chakra energy affects our ability to generate creative ideas, to make money, and to develop intimate relationships (even in business).

Chakra 3: Solar Plexus – The solar plexus chakra is concerned with our personal power and balanced control. Blockages in this chakra may materialize in the body as arthritis, ulcers, colon issues, diabetes, digestion, and adrenal issues. Stuck third chakra energy affects our self-esteem, our decision-making ability, our willingness to become a thought leader (or even to start our own business), and to take a stand for what we believe in.

Chakra 4: Heart – The heart chakra is concerned with our ability to give and receive love, in our personal as well as business life. Blockages in this chakra may materialize in the body as heart issues, circulatory problems, lung or breathing conditions, maladies of the breast or imbalance in the thymus gland. Stuck fourth chakra energy affects our ability to relate lovingly to our clients and staff, to receive the appreciation of colleagues and clients who enjoy and benefit from our work, to hold the space for self-discovery (if in the coaching, therapy, facilitator or other helping profession), and to engage in regular self-care.

Chakra 5: Throat – The throat chakra is concerned with our ability to authentically speak our truth and communicate from our heart. Blockages in this chakra may materialize in the body as colds, sore throat, laryngitis, thyroid issues, or neck, mouth and teeth problems. Stuck fifth chakra energy affects our ability to confidently communicate what we believe (e.g., in presentations or in delivering coaching or consulting or other services – or in our business philosophy), define our niche/brand, say no to customers that are not a fit for us, write our book, deliver presentations, and appear on the media or other venues to promote our business.

Chakra 6: Third Eye – The third eye chakra is concerned with our access to our intuition and/or psychic awareness. Blockages in this chakra may materialize in the body as brain conditions, nervous system imbalances, eye/ear/nose problems, and challenges with the pineal or pituitary gland. Stuck sixth chakra energy affects our self-image, our ability to develop unique content received via intuition, to channel or do spiritual readings (if so guided), to sell and market (heeding intuitive hunches) and to receive inner guidance regarding problems we face.

Chakra 7: Crown – The crown chakra is concerned with our direct connection to God or Higher Source. Blockages in this chakra may materialize in the body as muscular/skeletal issues, skin disorders, energy issues and chronic fatigue, and light/sound sensitivity. Stuck seventh chakra energy affects our ability to feel connected to our business spiritually, to find our life purpose, and to receive inspired guidance.

The following chart summarizes the business areas affected by each chakra and the physical symptoms which may indicate a blockage:

Chakra	Color	Focus	Physical Indications of Blockage	Business Areas Affected
1 – root	Red	Tribe; groundedness; family beliefs and heritage	Low back pain, sciatica, depression, immune disorders	Startup; getting basic financial needs met; building true tribe (vs. anonymous customers)
2 – sacral	Orange	Creativity, money, sex	Lower/mid back pain; ob-gyn issues; urinary issues	Revenue generation; expense control; idea generation

3 – solar plexus	Yellow	Personal power	Arthritis, ulcers, colon issues, diabetes, digestion, adrenals	Adopting the mindset of being a thought leader, entrepreneur; building a business vs. just offering a service
4 – heart	Green	Love (and heart of the body and energy system – no pun intended!). Its electromagnetic field is 5000 times more powerful than that of the brain!	Heart, circulation, lungs, shoulders, breasts, thymus	Ability to relate to clients; to hold deep regard for clients, staff; holding the coaching space; engaging in regular self-care
5 – throat	Lt blue	Authentic communication (blending heart and intuition/ chakras 4, 6)	Colds, sore throat, thyroid issues, neck, mouth, teeth, parathyroid, laryngitis	Speaking your truth; defining your niche/ brand; firing people you need to fire (clients or staff); being willing to polarize your audience; writing your book, speaking, spreading your message
6 – third eye	Indigo	Intuition, psychic awareness	Brain, nervous system, eye/ ears, nose, pineal, pituitary	Healthy self-image; receiving Inspired inspiration about client issues, program ideas, answers to challenges
7 – crown	Purple	Direct connection to God/Source	Muscular/ skeletal issues, skin, energetic disorders, light/sound sensitivity, chronic fatigue	Business may do well financially but you will feel disconnected from it – this is the receptor for defining your path and purpose

HOW TO IDENTIFY AND CLEAR AN ENERGY BLOCKAGE

Once you become aware that you are experiencing a blockage, take these steps:

1. Notice where your results are blocked – how is this issue manifesting?

2. Notice if you have had any physical symptoms that coincide with the onset of this issue.

3. Pay attention to any dreams, daydreams, or seemingly unusual urges (e.g., your money flow is blocked and you feel drawn to find the guitar you used to play and begin playing again). They can hold the pathway (even if it's a side door!) to clearing that block.

4. Refer to the chart above to see which chakra is connected to the issue.

5. Follow your intuition to begin (or resume) any activities you feel led to do that may begin to fill the energy.

6. Do an energy clearing visualization (see end of chapter) to remove the block and clear the way for your full expression!

A few years ago when I was in one of those places, I was drawn to get a set of acrylic paints and start painting. Immediately I resisted the idea: I had tried to become an artist in college, took all the right classes – and was all but asked to leave because I just didn't have the knack for it! So I had a bit of emotional baggage around the whole idea – but I decided to get the paints for myself as a birthday present anyway, and started dabbling with them. It was great fun! I played with doing multi-media pieces, metaphysical themes, and just abstract, colorful art that made me feel good. It had no motivation behind it other than having fun. And guess what? My finances resumed their flow too. I believe the two were connected. And when I coach people who feel financially blocked, inevitably they also face blockages in the other two issues. Choosing a creative outlet that feels good to them helps them be more successful in their business venture – and their relationships too!

VISUALIZATION TO CLEAR ENERGY BLOCKS

Use the following process to clear, rebalance or strengthen your connection through one of your chakras:

Sit comfortably in a chair with your feet flat on the floor and your eyes closed. Take 2 or 3 deep breaths, imagining you are breathing in through the bottom of your feet and all the way up through your body, creating a circle on the exhale back through the bottom of your feet. Consciously relax any areas of tension.

Bring your attention to the center of your stomach area, where the eternal life of your soul exists, like the pilot light of a furnace. Allow this light to expand to fill your entire body and being now, and to surround you with the white light of protection. Also envision a cord of light extending from the base of your spine into the center of the earth.

Now, bring to mind the area of your life or business that feels stuck or not quite as you would like it to be. Do you feel any tightness or tingling anywhere in your body as you bring this to mind? If you are already aware of a physical symptom that is connected to this issue, focus your attention gently there now.

Allow the white light to dissolve away any shadow, darkness or debris around the area where you feel the disease, tightness or tingling – and let the residue drop down through the grounding cord into the center of the earth, where it is immediately consumed in the magma of the earth's core.

Let yourself sit quietly in the peaceful acceptance that this blockage is gone now. In its place, allow Archangel Raphael to comfort that area of your body with soothing, green gel-like energy. Then, choose an empowering affirmation that you wish to implant where the old blockage was, such as
"I fully embody my Inspired essence now, and express it freely throughout my work and life."

Gently bring your attention back to the room, move your hands and feet and open your eyes.

20

TRANSFORMING SABOTAGING OR OUTDATED BELIEFS OF EACH INSPIRED SUCCESS PATH

Lisa, an Inspired Success Path 8-6, entered the field of business after college and advanced quickly, becoming a Vice President by her mid 30's. Attractive and intelligent, she was liked by most everyone, not only for her wonderful listening and problem-solving abilities, but for her commitment to be firm when required. In private, however, Lisa suffered silently. She doubted her true talents, and kept fearing someone would "find out" that she wasn't really as talented as she appeared to be. She continued to support her alcoholic mother financially, although it represented a hardship for Lisa given her other financial needs. Her mother had berated and talked down to her all of Lisa's life.

Lisa is a classic example of someone with natural talent for business leadership and financial success dealing with the third of our types of blocks to full expression of our Inspired Success Path: a sabotaging belief that "I'm not good enough" that compromised her ability to enjoy her success.

HOW BELIEFS BECOME EMBEDDED

Both the process of storing energy from unresolved past experiences in our chakras and the process of developing our belief system about life, people, and business are done unconsciously. We don't deliberately say to ourselves, "I think I'll store some blocked energy around this," or "I think I'll absorb this belief that I'm not good enough." But it happens, out of an instinctual need to protect ourselves from pain and, in the case of beliefs, from having to recreate a new belief every time a similar situation arises. The problem is the protection we form also insulates us from letting the good we desire in following that event.

Up to 70 percent of our beliefs are formed before we are 5 years old. The problem is, most people don't stop to re-examine the beliefs they embedded in their infancy and "update the software" in their unconscious realm. So the beliefs that are governing their adult life have long become outdated and often need to be re-examined. Fear is at the root of many of our sabotaging and outdated beliefs.

COMMON SABOTAGING BELIEFS FOR EACH INSPIRED SUCCESS PATH (ISP)

Each Inspired Success Path has its own common beliefs – stemming from the negative expression of that Path's energy – with which they grapple. If yours are not among those listed, follow your own inner guidance and intuition – this list is not exhaustive. And use the 5-step process below to reprogram yourself in that area so that your beliefs serve you, rather than sabotaging you.

INSPIRED SUCCESS PATH NUMBER 1

Those with an ISP 1 often struggle with beliefs about their worthiness to be leaders, their self-worth, powerlessness, fitting in, and control issues.

INSPIRED SUCCESS PATH NUMBER 2

Those with an ISP 2 often struggle with beliefs about their ability to deal with conflict, co-dependence, and losing themselves in other people's worlds.

INSPIRED SUCCESS PATH NUMBER 3

Those with an ISP 3 often struggle with beliefs about whether their ideas will be accepted, whether other people will accept them, and commitment issues.

INSPIRED SUCCESS PATH NUMBER 4

Those with an ISP 4 often struggle with beliefs about not being able to figure out how things work, unworthiness to create something lasting, and negative consequences from not following the rules.

INSPIRED SUCCESS PATH NUMBER 5

Those with an ISP 5 often struggle with beliefs about missing out on something (resulting in commitment issues), being limited or hemmed in, and fear of change.

INSPIRED SUCCESS PATH NUMBER 6

Those with an ISP 6 often struggle with beliefs about whether their needs are important (since they give so much to those they nurture and care for), how much is too much responsibility, and what will happen if a close friend or family member leaves them.

INSPIRED SUCCESS PATH NUMBER 7

Those with an ISP 7 often struggle with beliefs about trust of life, fear of meaninglessness, and worthiness to be in relationship.

INSPIRED SUCCESS PATH NUMBER 8

Those with an ISP 8 often struggle with beliefs about losing control, power or authority; their ability to keep the money they earn, and self-confidence.

INSPIRED SUCCESS PATH NUMBER 9

Those with an ISP 9 often struggle with beliefs about their connection to God and to humanity, expression of emotions and the deep philosophical ideas they have, and what will happen if the world's problems don't get solved.

INSPIRED SUCCESS PATH NUMBER 11

Those with an ISP 11 often struggle with beliefs about worthiness to deliver the spiritual message they have been given, fear of rejection for their ideas, and issues regarding conflict.

INSPIRED SUCCESS PATH NUMBER 22

Those with an ISP 22 often struggle with beliefs about not being able to figure out how to improve the things that matter to them, unworthiness to create something lasting, and negative consequences from not following the rules.

5 STEPS TO TRANSFORMING A BELIEF

When you suspect you are dealing with a sabotaging or outdated belief, the following five steps will help you change it.

1. Write out the current active belief (e.g., "I do not believe I deserve to earn $1 million.").

2. List the beliefs that support that core belief (e.g., "Rich people are selfish," "Money doesn't grow on trees," "People like me don't get rich").

3. List the beliefs that are opposite of your current beliefs – that is, the beliefs that someone would hold who had the traits or was in the situation you desire (e.g., "I deserve to be wealthy; I can earn $1 million this year.").

4. Identify the emotional vibration or feeling associated with that belief. (E.g., you may associate joy with wealth)

5. Use consistent repetition of the new beliefs to reprogram your subconscious through affirmations, visualization, and similar processes. Write it on sticky-notes and post them on your mirror, your desk, and refrigerator – anywhere you will see them regularly. Repeat the belief to yourself frequently. Envision your life the way it will be when the new belief is fully integrated. Or create a screensaver for your computer with the belief written on it. Be sure to repeatedly feel the

emotion that represents the new belief – it is the fuel that brings your new belief alive in all of its aspects.

Within 21 to 30 days, your new belief will be as natural to you then as your current one is now!

PART FIVE:

DOING BUSINESS BY THE NUMBERS

In this Part, we will explore how Business Numerology can be applied in key areas of your day-to-day business activities, including:

- Choosing Your Business Name and Start-up Date
- Identifying Your Ideal Market
- Leveraging Your Zone of Excellence
- Choosing Staff or Team Members

21

CHOOSING YOUR BUSINESS NAME, START-UP DATE AND MORE BY THE NUMBERS

Business Numerology can be used not only for learning more about your personal gifts, talents, and business/career choice – but also to name your business and products, choose your start-up date, bank account or phone number, and much more! If you choose these important aspects of your business so that they align with their vibration as revealed through numerology, they will be much more likely to embody success and desirable outcomes – and to avoid many setbacks and challenges.

I used numerology to name my new business, Your Divine Gifts – as well as this book! The name denotes, among other things, that through it, one can do anything, is extremely capable, and a true survivor. It is also highly flexible, can adapt to new circumstances quickly, and has excellent reflexes; often, important decisions are made in seconds, seemingly impulsively even. But due to sharp intuition and even sharper intelligence, those decisions are almost always right on the money. This name draws people who want things to be "different," and don't like the tried and proven.

Any business name can be analyzed to determine its key meaning through numerology. For example, Google is a 22/4 Life Path, the Master Builder – and look what it has created as a structure that has changed the world! It is key to know what energy your business name carries too.

BUSINESS NAME ANALYSIS: IS YOUR NAME IN ALIGNMENT AND FAVORABLE?

Just as your name expresses a vibration unique to you, your business name does too. Of most interest is the name itself, though its "birthday" (the legal date of formation OR the day the domain or online presence was made public) sets its life path too.

It can be favorable – but not always advisable - to have a business name with the same Life Path number as yours. For example, Steve Jobs and the company he co-founded, Apple Computer, both have a 1 birthday or Life Purpose number. (Indeed, he was born with a 10/1 Life Path, the Wheel of Fortune – so he brought no Karmic Debt with him.) This alignment of his life path with his company's brought industry leadership and long-term proven results to both him and the company. (We would need to look at the Personal Year Numbers and other factors in the profile to see the numerological reason behind the eventual setbacks – including Steve being fired from and rehired years later into the company!).

To get the value of your business name, you will simply add the energy of each letter together and reduce to a single digit:

1	2	3	4	5	6	7	8	9
A	B	C	D	E	F	G	H	I
J	K	L	M	N	O	P	Q	R
S	T	U	V	W	X	Y	Z	

Be sure to give your intuition some credit too in choosing your business name! If you have two or three that are equally appropriate, which one do you like best? As long as it has a favorable vibration and is compatible with your profile, you can trust it!

In addition to the vibration of the full name (the "Dominant Vibration"), it is wise to also review the Vowel Vibration and the Base Vibration of the name – and how the three vibrations interact – to get a full picture of the business name's impact and energy.

Here are a few guidelines about what vibration is best for certain types of businesses:

- Advertising, promotional and publishing businesses: 3, 5, 6, 8

- Arts businesses: 2, 3, 6, 9

- Educational businesses: 3, 6, 7, 9

- Entrepreneurial businesses: 1, 8

- Financial businesses: 6, 8, 9

- Health-related businesses: 2, 4, 7

- Product businesses: 2, 4, 8

- Research businesses: 2, 7, 9

- Service businesses: 2, 3, 6, 9

- Technology businesses: 1, 3, 6, 7, 9

If your business is a sole proprietorship, the Expression and Destiny numbers should align with yours.

If you are forming (or have formed) a partnership, both partners' energy should be compared with that of the business in choosing the name. The three families of Inspired Success Paths discussed in chapter 2 can come into play here.

And for financial success, generally the numbers 1, 6, 8 and 9 are considered more favorable than the other numbers.

You can also consult numerology for product and program names, to ensure that the vibration matches the essential benefits and description of the product or program, and the company's overall mission and soul's purpose.

(Note: a detailed analysis of your business name is available through our web site: www.yourInspiredgifts.com/numerology-readings)

USING NUMEROLOGY TO CHOOSE YOUR BANK ACCOUNT, PHONE NUMBER, ADDRESS AND MORE

Whenever you are involved in a transaction involving numbers – and you will begin to notice that they are everywhere! – pay attention to the numbers involved. What vibration and energy does this number bring to that situation?

Here are some of the number-related aspects of business where you will want to add the sum of the digits involved (and consult their meaning as outlined in this book) before you finalize your selection:

- Bank account number (aim for an 8 total for financial prosperity)

- Phone number (aim for an 8 or a number identical to your business's Life Path, counting the area code and the 7 additional digits)

- Street address of the building where your business is located (even if you work at home, run the numerology on your address to see what vibration is active there)

- Suite number or other unit number within the building where your business is located

- Credit card number

- Federal and state tax identification numbers

Also look for trends among the digits of each number. Does your phone number have more than 4 of one number? If so that vibration may be multiplied in your life – especially if it appears in your core numbers or in other aspects of your business!

6 8 4
2 1 5 7
9 0 3 3

22

LEVERAGING YOUR ZONE OF EXCELLENCE AND CHOOSING YOUR MARKET BY THE NUMBERS

You know from determining your Inspired Success Path the types of gifts and talents you have, as well as the channel through which to express them. However, another aspect of the numerology profile – the "Planes of Expression" – allow us to get even more specific about whether you are more likely to excel in areas involving physical, mental, emotional or intuitive tasks.

THE FOUR DIMENSIONS OF YOUR GIFTS: YOUR PLANES OF EXPRESSION

The channels through which you express your Life Path, Expression, Heart's Desire, Personality and Maturity Number include the physical, the mental, the emotional, and the intuitive. And depending on which of these is strongest will help fill in some of the "missing pieces" regarding your business focus and the parts of your business that are best for you to personally do – versus delegate.

To determine your Planes of Expression, each letter of the alphabet is assigned a category among the four (physical, mental, emotional and intuitive). The percentage of each category in your name is an indicator of which of these Planes is strongest, and which is weakest. A final variable is whether the letters are "creative," "vacillating," or "grounded" in nature.

This area of numerology is somewhat complex, but we can outline the basics here – and if you wish a full reading including the four Planes of Expression, feel free to contact us through our web site at www. YourDivineGifts.com.

In your profile, a number is assigned as the energy value for each Plane. The numbers here have the essential elements of the vibration of each (1-9 and 11) discussed in previous chapters. For example, if one had a 1 Physical Plane of Expression, it would say that they have a strong personality, are active in life and take the lead in business and other situations (the leadership traits of the 1). If one had a 4 in Emotional Plane of Expression, it might mean that they disliked the unpredictability of emotions and would try to contain them – since 4's like structure.

Here is an example of the number of the letters of your name that are in each of the 4 Planes, the number that are creative vs. vacillating vs. grounded, and what that means in terms of strengths and weaknesses, using the name Thomas John Hancock:

	CREATIVE		VACILLLATING		GROUNDED		TOTAL	
	# of letters	value	# of letters	value	# of letters	value	# of letters	value
Physical					M	4	1	4
Mental	AA	2	HJHNHN	8			8	1
Emotional	OOO	9	TS	3			5	3
Intuitive	K	2			CC	6	3	8
	6	4	8	11	3	1	17	7

To increase your self-awareness, consider how you approach tasks requiring each of the 4 Planes. What does the energy number of each Plane tell you?

ACHIEVING EXCELLENCE BY APPLYING THE PLANES OF EXCELLENCE

To excel in your Inspired Success Path, you will want most of your primary responsibilities to be within that Plane. Following are representative business functions and the primary Plane involved with that function:

Business Function	Physical	Mental	Emotional	Intuitive
Accounting		x		
Administrative assistant		x		
Advertising				x
Bookkeeping		x		
Coaching, counseling		x	x	x
Computer programming		x		x
Copywriting		x		x

Business Function	Physical	Mental	Emotional	Intuitive
Customer service		x	x	
Data entry		x		
Employee counseling			x	
Event planning	x	x		
Financial Management		x		
Graphic design			x	x
Janitorial services	x			
Legal representation		x		
Manufacturing/ production	x			
Marketing		x		x
Operations management	x	x	x	
Product fulfillment	x			
Product sales	x			x
Quality control	x	x		
Research		x		x
Service sales		x		x
Social media updates		x		
Speaking, presentations	x			
Strategic planning		x		
Telephone answering	x		x	
Trade shows	x			
Travel planning	x	x		
Web design		x		x

CHOOSING YOUR IDEAL MARKET/TRIBE BY THE NUMBERS

Every business owner must define the ideal market – or what we now refer to as a "tribe" sharing a common challenge – on which to target their outreach. In the past, this was often done by an "outside-in" method, by which the company surveyed the market to determine which industries were growing (and therefore more likely to buy from them) and focusing on that group.

In the current climate, dominated as it is by service businesses – many of whom are entrepreneurs – an "inside-out" approach can provide a better starting point. It's not that we want to ignore the marketplace. But by delving into one's Inspired Success Path (and that of their business), we can see the natural markets for each of them, since each will tend to attract people who are lacking the primary talents that Inspired Success Path embodies. Then, we can follow that by refining our definition by examining the external market and clarifying their needs, as well as the way they prefer to receive the kind of solution the business provides.

Following are the natural markets for each of the Inspired Success Paths.

NATURAL MARKETS FOR INSPIRED SUCCESS PATH NUMBER 1

Because ISP 1's bring natural leadership skills, confidence, and the ability to start new projects to their business, they tend to attract people who are passionate but lack confidence. They long to be leaders but aren't sure how to get started or what to do to achieve their goals.

NATURAL MARKETS FOR INSPIRED SUCCESS PATH NUMBER 2

Because ISP 2's bring natural harmonizing, mediation and relationship skills to their business, they tend to attract people who feel isolated, disconnected, or in conflict with others. They long to develop sensitivity and bring harmony to their life – either internal harmony among their conflicting goals or external harmony to their relationships - but aren't sure how to accomplish it or what is required to cultivate these abilities.

NATURAL MARKETS FOR INSPIRED SUCCESS PATH NUMBER 3

Because ISP 3's bring natural creativity and communication skills to their business, they tend to attract people who are linear thinkers, analytical, shy, or feel bound to follow the rules at any cost. They long to be more creative and speak their truth but aren't sure how to get started or what to do to achieve this.

NATURAL MARKETS FOR INSPIRED SUCCESS PATH NUMBER 4

Because ISP 4's bring natural organizational and process skills, dedication and hard work to their business, they tend to attract people who are passionate but lack structure. They long to become organized, but aren't sure how to get started or what to do to achieve their goals.

NATURAL MARKETS FOR INSPIRED SUCCESS PATH NUMBER 5

Because ISP 5's bring natural change management, adaptability and exploration skills to their business, they tend to attract people who feel stuck, want to become more spontaneous, and color "inside the lines". They long to be adaptable and embrace change but don't know how to get started or what to do to loosen up and broaden their perspective.

NATURAL MARKETS FOR INSPIRED SUCCESS PATH NUMBER 6

Because ISP 6's bring natural nurturing, caring, responsibility and family orientation skills to their business, they tend to attract people who long to be more caring, to assume responsibility for their own life and destiny, or want to balance a business/work orientation with a family orientation. They long to bring balance to their lives but aren't sure how to get started or what to do to achieve their goals.

NATURAL MARKETS FOR INSPIRED SUCCESS PATH NUMBER 7

Because ISP 7's bring natural research, analytical and/or spiritual/intuitive gifts to their business, they tend to attract people who are either skimming the surface of many topics and want to learn to focus, or who are strictly linear/analytical thinkers and are now sensing spiritual gifts emerging. They long to delve deeper into their area of interest, but don't know how to avoid their approach of being scattered.

NATURAL MARKETS FOR INSPIRED SUCCESS PATH NUMBER 8

Because ISP 8's bring natural business, financial and authority to their business, they tend to attract people who are passionate but lack confidence, the ability to manage money, or the ability to exercise their own personal power. They long to be successful in business and/or investments but aren't sure how to get started or what to do to achieve their goals.

NATURAL MARKETS FOR INSPIRED SUCCESS PATH NUMBER 9

Because ISP 9's bring natural transformational, humanitarian, and teaching skills to their business, they tend to attract people who have a passion for change but feel their vision is too big to be achieved. They long to be a transformational influence in their community – or the world – but aren't sure how to get started or what to do to achieve their lofty goals.

NATURAL MARKETS FOR INSPIRED SUCCESS PATH NUMBER 11

Because ISP 11's bring natural spiritual insights, the ability to see internal connections between people and things, and inspiration to their business, they tend to attract people who are just awakening to their spiritual nature and want a guide on the journey. They long to make a bigger impact but aren't sure how to integrate their spiritual self into the pursuit of their goals.

NATURAL MARKETS FOR INSPIRED SUCCESS PATH NUMBER 22

Because ISP 22's bring natural visioning, project management and follow-through skills their business, they tend to attract people who have a sense of what they want to accomplish, but are disorganized or lack the ability to turn their dream into reality. They long to be successful but don't know how to organize their efforts toward their desired outcome.

Knowing your market is an important next step. Then, you need to ensure your team members (whether employees or contractors) are aligned with (1) your company's Inspired Success Path, and (2) the tasks, roles and responsibilities you want them to perform. Our next chapter addresses this key issue.

$$6\ 8\ 4$$
$$2\ 1\ 5\ 7$$
$$9\ 0\ 3$$

23

CHOOSING STAFF BY THE NUMBERS

What if you could lean the odds in favor of a successful working relationship with the staff you hire or contract services to? And ensure that they are well-suited to your company and to the role for which they are being hired? You can with Business Numerology!

There are two ways to apply Business Numerology in staffing:

1. Determine which areas of the business (or your area of responsibility if you are a manager or executive within a company) you should delegate, based on the weak areas in your Planes of Expression

2. Choose staff based on whether their Inspired Success Path fits the position you wish to fill

WHAT YOUR PLANES OF EXPRESSION MEAN FOR DELEGATING

If you find that your strongest Plane of Expression is in the Physical, with many letters of your name in that category (using the chart in chapter 22), you will want to be an action person in your business. Doing things, in a direct and physical manner, is what Physical Plane people do best. Whether it is athletics, cooking, building, or any other physical activity, your exact Expression number energy (1-9, 11 or 22) will help you determine in which physical arena to focus. If your Physical Plane is low or lacking, delegate those tasks to others.

If you find that your strongest Plane of Expression is in the Mental, with many letters of your name in that category, you will want to analyze, think, make decisions, determine what is best, and look beneath the surface for the true meaning. You are a great strategist and visionary as well. Your exact Expression number energy (1-9, 11 or 22) will help you determine in which mental arena to focus. If your Mental Plane is low or lacking, delegate those tasks to others.

If you find that your strongest Plane of Expression is in the Emotional, with many letters of your name in that category, you will tend to react with deep feelings to what happens in your life and business. You can follow your heart where it leads, and are a great comfort to others because of this emotional nature. Counseling, coaching, acting and other fields that require strong emotions are a great fit. Your exact Expression number energy (1-9, 11 or 22) will help you determine in which emotional arena to focus. If your Emotional Plane is low or lacking, delegate those tasks to others.

If you find that your strongest Plane of Expression is in the Intuitive, with many letters of your name in that category, you are a rare person indeed! You may have psychic abilities, and will have a "gut feel" about situations and people you encounter. Being the person the company comes to in validating any important decisions, feeling their way to new directions, and the like are a good fit for the Intuitive

Plane person. Your exact Expression number energy (1-9, 11 or 22) will help you determine in which intuitive arena to focus. If your Intuitive Plane is low or lacking, delegate those tasks to others.

WHAT PROFILE IS BEST FOR WHAT STAFF MEMBER?

Once you decide to outsource or delegate a task or role, consider what energy would be best for them to align with both you and their responsibilities.

Consider this summary of each number's energy in general:

Number	Key Words and Concepts
1	Leadership, independence, innovation, making a start, taking charge
2	Cooperation, peacemaking, harmony, unity, relationships
3	Creative communication, creative expression, social magnet, imagination, optimism, playfulness
4	Structure, foundation, building, hard work, formation, endurance, seriousness, practicality
5	Change, travel, adaptability, transition, progressive thinking, resourcefulness, freedom, versatility
6	Nurturing, home/hearth, service, balance, responsibility, domestic
7	Research, study, analysis, loner, metaphysical pursuits, science, technology, solitude, studying, wisdom, spiritual focus, investigative, mystical
8	Business success, power, authority, finance, business, success, material wealth, organization
9	Philanthropist, humanitarian, vision, transformation, spiritual consciousness, cosmic, teaching, global awareness, perfection

Master numbers:	
11	Spiritual Messenger, inspirational, psychic, consciousness-raising, world reformer
22	Master Builder, visionary, large-scale planner, global transformational catalyst

Now you can calculate (or have us do a full profile) the Inspired Success Path of each candidate and match to their role. Here are some representative examples:

Position	Inspired Success Path
Accountant	4 or 7
Administrative assistant	2, 3 or 4
Advertising executive	3
Bookkeeper	4 or 7
Chaplain	7, 11
Computer programmer	4
Copywriter	3
Customer service representative	4, 6
Data entry clerk	4
Employee counselor	2, 5, 6
Event planner	3
Executive	1, 8
Financial Manager	4, 8
Graphic designer	3, 4, 7
Janitor	6, 7
Lawyer	1, 4, 8
Manufacturing/production worker	4
Marketing professional	3, 6, 8

Minister	2, 3, 6, 7, 11
Operations manager	4, 6, 8
Product sales representative	1, 2, 3, 4, 8
Psychic or intuitive reader	7, 11
Quality control manager	1, 4, 7, 8
Researcher	7
Service sales representative	1, 2, 3, 8
Social media specialist	3, 6, 9
Strategist	1, 8, 11
Technology inventor	22
Telephone answering receptionist	2, 3
Trainer	1, 3, 4, 8
Travel agent	5
Web designer	3, 4, 7

Using Business Numerology in your staffing, delegating and strategic planning will significantly improve staff effectiveness, morale, and your own satisfaction level as you let go of areas in which you are weak. All that remains is to forecast the timing of key events in your business and align with the natural order – which we will do in Part Six.

PART SIX:

THE RHYTHM OF YOUR SUCCESS

In this Part, we will explore how to use Business Numerology in timing and forecasting both your personal life events and your business launches and other key dates, including:

- The 4 Pinnacles and Challenges of Your Life and of Your Business

- The Personal Year Number for You and the Business

- What Activities Are Best Suited to Each Personal Year and Month

24

THE CYCLES OF LIFE AND BUSINESS

YOUR FOUR PINNACLES – OR STAGES OF YOUR LIFE

During the course of your life, you undergo *four stages or long-term cycles* we call Pinnacles in numerology. They vary in length, and each guides you to your highest attainment, or what is possible for us to achieve during that period. When you transition from one Pinnacle to another, you often experience a substantial shift in your life, since the shift occurs in a Personal Year 1 or 9. I met my husband (whom I have been with for more than 20 years) at the transition from my first to second Pinnacle, graduated from coaching school and started Career Coach Institute at the transition from my second to third Pinnacle, and I moved to Scottsdale and entered a new line of work – and new group of friends – when my third Pinnacle gave way to my fourth.

Knowing your Pinnacles in advance can help you be ready for this! This is one of several forecasting elements in the numerology profile – the Personal Year (which we look at later in the chapter) being another.

Think of the Pinnacles as themes for that part of your life. The first one is one of the longest, lasting from birth to our late 20's or early 30's (depending on the variables of your unique profile); the second is the time of blossoming and lasts 9 years, as does the third which focuses on middle age and maturity, and the fourth – harvest cycle - encompasses the remainder of your life.

Each Pinnacle has its own unique energy, computed through a numerology formula. And while it does not tell us whether to do something or avoid doing something – as a Personal Year or Personal Month will – it does tell us what the goal and/or lesson is that you have, at a soul level, intended to accomplish during that period of your life.

Every business also has the energy of at least one Pinnacle (that applicable based on their month and day of formation – see below), but unless the business lasts more than 28 years the additional three Pinnacles will not come into play.

HOW TO CALCULATE YOUR PINNACLES

The formula for each Pinnacle is different. They are calculated as follows:

Pinnacle	Formula	Length
1	Month of birth + day of birth	36 – Life Path
2	Day of birth + year of birth	9 years
3	First Pinnacle + Second Pinnacle	9 years
4	Month of birth + year of birth	Rest of lifetime

Determine yours now:

Pinnacle	Formula	Length	Ages
1	Month of birth + day of birth	36 – Life Path	
2	Day of birth + year of birth	9 years	
3	First Pinnacle + Second Pinnacle	9 years	
4	Month of birth + year of birth	Rest of lifetime	

THE MEANING OF EACH PINNACLE

1 PINNACLE

During the 1 Pinnacle, you will reach for independence, individuality, and self-reliance. You are learning to stand on your own two feet, to set your own course. As part of learning this lesson, you may be required to bounce back after a setbacks or challenges. If you can stay focused on your goals, you will successfully navigate this Pinnacle. During the 1 Pinnacle, you will experience a great deal of personal growth. Leadership, management, and taking charge of your own destiny are traits of this Pinnacle.

You will attract teachers and other companions and experiences that will help you develop these traits. Willpower is a valuable tool in this Pinnacle, since you will find little support from family and friends during this time. Indeed, you discover what you are truly made of when you are in a 1 Pinnacle! When placed in your third or fourth phase of life, this Pinnacle indicates you are being groomed for leadership. Be careful not to become too self-righteous, self-centered or stubborn. Others will help you – if you let them.

2 PINNACLE

During the 2 Pinnacle, the focus is on developing harmonious relationships while sustaining a sense of self. Collaboration, patience, teamwork, and inner awareness are all traits to be cultivated during a 2 Pinnacle. It's the opposite of the 1 Pinnacle: independence is not called for here. The quest is not only for harmony with others, but within the self as well.

The 2 Pinnacle helps you cultivate sensitivity to others and their needs, as well as ways to be supportive. You will learn to see both sides of any situation and to bring people into harmony, cooperation and collaboration. You may also find your feelings get hurt more easily than normal, so reach out for comfort and support from others! In addition, you may find you have increased interest in creating beauty around you, in music, and in the arts.

3 PINNACLE

During the 3 Pinnacle, you will awaken your creative expression – either for the first time or in new ways. It is important during a 3 Pinnacle to refine your artistic abilities – or perhaps even pursue a creative career. Your imagination, as well as your social skills, will be actively cultivated during this Pinnacle. You will learn to inspire others, to encourage them, and to share your life experiences through captivating stories.

You will find your energy upbeat and positive, with interests in many things – so discipline is called for. You will attract new friends and associates during this period. Just be careful not to scatter your energy, but exercise the amount of discipline that is required to channel your energies and interests in one or two primary outlets. Beware impulsiveness, overspending, and overindulging in physical pleasures.

4 PINNACLE

The 4 Pinnacle is a time of hard work and building a foundation – in family or work – for the future. The efforts that go into this Pinnacle will yield dividends in the future. This a time of learning how things work, working within timelines, discovering how to manage money and resources.

By bringing your ideas into form during the 4 Pinnacle, you will establish the framework for your future pursuits. People will come to depend on you for advice, support, and implementation. There is a danger of becoming too serious and work-focused during this time, so cultivate some time for leisure. Creativity may be curtailed during this period, as you develop the rules, systems, structures and procedures required to bring your dreams to life.

5 PINNACLE

During the 5 Pinnacle, expect to have change and uncertainty emerge. You may feel restless – even in what used to satisfy you – or change may be thrust upon you repeatedly by life circumstances. This can feel unsettling – especially if your 5 is in one of the longer Pinnacles. You are likely to find yourself traveling, pursuing adventures, and seeking new experiences. Career changes, starting a business, or at least significant shifts in focus or role within your current profession or career are likely.

It can be tempting to keep jumping from one thing to another, avoiding settling down, during this Pinnacle. But its lesson is to choose carefully – after sampling the options – and begin to put roots down in your chosen field (or relationship). Your writing and communication abilities will become stronger during this Pinnacle too. Avoid the temptation to make hasty decisions – instead, adapt to the changes as they come and find your place within them.

6 PINNACLE

The 6 Pinnacle brings a focus on family, home, and responsibility to loved ones. You will usually find yourself caring for others (whether people or pets!). Your nurturing may be called for due to a troubled teen, a sudden illness or disease of a family member, or other similar circumstances. You may feel drawn to do community outreach, and to beautify your home, office, or other environment.

You will need to learn to balance giving and receiving during this time so you do not become resentful of the demands of others. Simply accept the burdens and responsibilities that have been given to you, get help when you can, and bring the joy of care, comfort and nurturing to those close to you.

7 PINNACLE

During the 7 Pinnacle, you will find yourself learning and reflecting much more than in other periods, and you may also be undergoing soul development and cultivating spiritual gifts. Plan on taking more time alone than normal – you will need it to study, analyze, and integrate what you feel drawn to study at this time. As a result, you may develop some unique wisdom for which people will pay you (e.g., through an invention, starting a business, career recognition or academic/research publication).

When the 7 Pinnacle occurs in the first stage of life, you may feel isolated and different from other people. You may also struggle to relate to others – especially emotionally. When it appears in a later stage of life, it often signals the awakening of spiritual quests for the meaning of life, and/or the emergence of spiritual or psychic gifts. Alternately, it can call you to deepen your knowledge and expertise in your chosen profession through additional study (e.g., going back to school).

Be careful not to isolate unduly or to become excessively critical. Explain to loved ones that you need the alone time to research, study or reflect, and to avoid taking it as a personal affront or indication you do not love them or wish to be with them.

8 PINNACLE

During the 8 Pinnacle, you will focus on the areas of business and finance, and exploring your own personal power. Financial rewards – as well as setbacks – are typical here as you develop sound judgment, management abilities, and authentic authority. It is known as the cycle of harvest – and rewards from the hard work of your past will emerge now. You may feel like you have the "Midas touch" as everything you apply your talents to prospers.

Avoid the temptation to focus solely on money – but instead focus on how it can be used for greater good – to make this Pinnacle more enjoyable. Also, the 8 Pinnacle can lead to excessive focus on work and finances to the exclusion of family. Remember they are important too! This Pinnacle helps you trust your own inner authority, and use power for the good of all.

9 PINNACLE

During the 9 Pinnacle, you are being called to find a focus, project or occupation that will further the greater good – not just your own personal interests. You will be sensitive to the needs of the planet, and will be able to inspire others with your heart-felt perspective on solutions to global problems. You will attract experiences to help you cultivate tolerance, compassion, love and selflessness. Love for your fellow human is called for, and you will be asked to think beyond yourself to that which will better the planet.

Emotional crises are common (since this is also a time of releasing that which no longer works). Use them as a gateway to your greater purpose. Since 9 is the number of completion, there are inevitable endings during this Pinnacle – which makes it more difficult than some. And don't let your idealistic dreams and visions of the future cause you to become disillusioned when they don't immediately come into fruition.

11 PINNACLE

During an 11 Pinnacle, you may experience the Master Number energy of the Spiritual Messenger – if you are living from that vibration – or you may experience it as the 2 – the lower vibration. You will find yourself being highly sensitive, emotionally and intuitively, and will experience substantial spiritual growth.

Navigating the 11 Pinnacle can leave you feeling like you'd love to settle down and focus, but this Pinnacle's energy keeps you growing and learning new things. You know you are different from others, and that your gifts are extraordinary. But once you come to terms with the energy of this period, you may feel drawn to share your unique perspective through speaking, writing or in another way that will inspire and transform others.

22 PINNACLE

The 22 Pinnacle is quite rare, and usually only occurs after two cycles of the 11/2. Building on the change of consciousness during those stages, you are poised and ready to make change on a massive scale. There are both physical and spiritual challenges evident within this Pinnacle. However, there is also tremendous potential during this period.

You will create or invent something that transforms the world and leaves is permanently changed. And as you bring that special something to life, you capably manage the people, resources and details of the plan, drawing on the Master Number vibration of the 22/4 energy. Be careful to keep balance in your personal life, as the double 2 energy in this number can bring emotional sensitivity along with the big vision you hold.

YOUR 4 CHALLENGES IN LIFE

Each of the Pinnacles has a corresponding Challenge that accompanies it (lasting the same length of time). *These are issues that we need to conquer to complete our soul's evolution.* Knowing them can help us avoid the frustrations of similar issues arising again and again, as we understand the challenge that we are to master. They are not so much lessons or problems, but aspects of yourself to be integrated into who you are becoming through navigating that Challenge.

The exact issues within each Challenge will be the mirror image of the Pinnacle for that number. For example, whereas a 1 Pinnacle is all about cultivating independence and individuality, a 1 Challenge will be a time when you will have problems (or "opportunities") standing up for yourself and perhaps find yourself feeling unsupported so that you can overcome this Challenge.

Some people have a different energy in each Challenge; some have the same energy repeated in one or more. But knowing what they are can help you make sense of seemingly endless or ongoing problems in your life so that you can harvest their value for your soul's growth and evolution.

HOW TO CALCULATE THE CHALLENGES

The formula for each Challenge is different. They are calculated as follows:

Pinnacle	Formula	Length
1	Day of birth - month of birth	36 – Life Path
2	Year of birth - day of birth	9 years
3	Second Challenge – First Challenge	9 years
4	Year of birth - month of birth	Rest of lifetime

Calculate yours now:

Pinnacle	Formula	Length	Ages
1	Day of birth - month of birth	36 – Life Path	
2	Year of birth - day of birth	9 years	
3	Second Challenge – First Challenge	9 years	
4	Year of birth - month of birth	Rest of lifetime	

THE MEANING OF EACH CHALLENGE

1 CHALLENGE

During the 1 Challenge, you will be tested to stand up for yourself, to be independent, and to rely on yourself. You may be required to bounce back after a setbacks or challenges. If you can stay focused on your goals, you will successfully navigate this Challenge. During the 1 Challenge, you will experience a great deal of personal growth.

Leadership, management, and taking charge of your own destiny are called for in this Challenge.

2 CHALLENGE

During the 2 Challenge, the focus is on becoming sensitive to others and their needs. Some people experience low self-confidence or shyness during this Challenge. You are cautioned not to overgive to others, but to developing harmonious relationships while sustaining your sense of self. Collaboration, patience, teamwork, and inner awareness are all traits to be cultivated during a 2 Challenge.

3 CHALLENGE

During the 3 Challenge, you will have a tendency to be critical of yourself and others, and nothing you create will seem good enough. You may shy away from social interactions – and as a consequence feel alone and isolated. Get out of your shell, spend time with others, and dare to pursue the creative channels to which you feel drawn!

4 CHALLENGE

The 4 Challenge is a time of hard work and building a foundation – in family or work – for the future. You may feel constrained or limited by your job, your family dynamics, or other factors. This is to help you develop structure, discipline and focus. Avoid the tendency to leave projects unfished, to be disorganized, and to ignore the details. This Challenge is designed to help you reconcile yourself with the requirements of life, and put them into orderly application in your life.

5 CHALLENGE

During the 5 Challenge, you will feel drawn in many directions and experience constant change. You will feel drawn to mood-altering substances, physical pleasures, and anything that will give you a new experience – which can lead to addiction if not kept in check. Beware of the danger of becoming a persistent wanderer – jack of all trades, master of none – in your pursuit of the new or your wanderlust for foreign, exciting places. Find an area you enjoy and commit to it, and you will have learned the lesson of this Challenge.

6 CHALLENGE

The 6 Challenge focuses on family, home, and responsibility to loved ones – and you may feel burdened by the obligations thrust on you in that arena. You may find yourself in unhealthy relationships including codependency, abuse, or simply continuing to give of yourself with no reward or reciprocation. Unless you accept responsibility for those people and situations that are put in your life, this Challenge can be quite draining and even damaging.

7 CHALLENGE

During the 7 Challenge, you are suspicious and skeptical of new information (or people). You require proof, analysis and logical justification – which is not always available! You will find yourself being quite serious, even aloof and withdrawn, during this challenge, as you sort out what is true for you and what is not. Don't repress your true feelings – learn to identify and express them, and in turn let them be a companion to your intellectual strength.

8 CHALLENGE

During the 8 Challenge, you will have lessons in the areas of business, finance, and personal power. You may be obsessed with money and/or power, to the exclusion of other relationships, traits and priorities. The Challenge is to see more deeply into the true meaning of life – and business – and to put them in balance. Avoid the temptation to focus solely on money and power for their own sake, and instead see how they can be used for greater good. Also avoid giving your power away, as this simply sidesteps the lessons to be learned in this Challenge.

9 CHALLENGE

There is no 9 Challenge in numerology, since it is the highest number and all others are subtracted from it.

THE 0 CHALLENGE

The one difference between the Challenges and the Pinnacles is that there is a 0 Challenge in some charts, which usually indicates an old soul that has chosen to leave the exact issue to be worked on to be determined during the incarnation (i.e., lifetime) itself. It is a Challenge that provides opportunity for improving the world and its people in some way, and you will have repeated opportunities to serve others. It carries a great deal of responsibility.

The Pinnacles and Challenges give us the big picture view of our four life stages. Next, we look at the smaller cycles that run within them and can help you attune your activities to them.

25

USING BUSINESS NUMEROLOGY FOR FORECASTING AND PLANNING

One of the most fascinating uses of Business Numerology is its use in forecasting. By knowing the energy of the Personal Year, Personal Month, and even Personal Day you are experiencing, you can align your activities and plans with that vibration and enjoy greater success.

Does this mean you are destined or doomed to only do what is called for by that energy in a given year or month? No! But like the gardener who decides to plant his/her garden in the summer, the results you get by acting counter to that natural flow will not be the highest and best. Exercise your free will with care when it comes to challenging the energy of your Personal Year and Month!

Among the key events for which numerology can help through forecasting are:

- Changing jobs

- Starting a business

- Incorporating

- Opening a store

- Launching a product or program

- Closing a transaction by which you merge with or acquire another company

- Hiring staff

- Going on a road trip (for training, marketing, or public relations)

- Any other key events

YOUR PERSONAL YEAR

Within the context of your Pinnacles and Challenges, you will go through nine-year cycles throughout your life – as does your business. Each Personal Year has a unique energy – and you will go through them as many times 9 as you live. Each nine-year cycle is a growth stage, and the Personal Years within them are aspects of that stage.

Being aware of your Personal Year allows you to know what lies ahead for you in the coming year, and helps you prepare for any anticipated challenges that often go with that number. It is one of the most significant numbers to know if your intention is to become aligned with your soul's natural rhythm.

HOW TO CALCULATE YOUR PERSONAL YEAR

We begin by knowing the "Universal Year," derived by adding together the 4 digits of the current year. For example, to get the Universal Year for 2014, we would add 2 + 0 + 1 + 4 = Universal Year 7.

To determine your Personal Year, add your month of birth plus your day of birth to the Universal Year. So if you were born March 16, you would add 3 (March being the third month of the year) plus 1 + 6 = 7 to the Universal Year 7. 3 + 7 + 7 = 17, 1 + 7 = 8. So you would be in an 8 Personal Year.

Following is a summary of the energy within each Personal Year:

Personal Year	Energy
1	New start, taking the lead, initiating new projects (or even a new business), planting seeds
2	Relationships, sensitivity, cooperation
3	Creative ideas, social interaction, communication, inspiration
4	Hard work, building the structure for the future, bringing dreams into physical form, putting down roots, perseverance
5	Change, travel, unpredictability, transition, freedom, taking risks (and removing any blocks or stuckness from the 4 year)
6	Focus on family, caring for loved ones, and responsibility
7	Research, study, analysis, solitude, meditation, metaphysical pursuits, education
8	Business success, power, authority, finance, reward, recognition
9	Year of completion, transformation, release, and preparing for the next cycle

THE MEANING OF EACH PERSONAL YEAR

PERSONAL YEAR 1

Ready, set, go! This is the year to begin new projects, new relationships, and new businesses. You have the "green light" to pursue what interests and calls to you now. You will need a vision, a plan, and a dream – and this is the year to begin planting seeds to make it happen. If you have felt constrained or stifled in any way, now is the time to stand up for yourself, speak your truth and move forward with confidence. You can turn the spotlight on yourself to reflect on what you want, where you are going, and how to get there. If you need to make personal changes such as to your appearance, the energy supports you in making those changes now.

PERSONAL YEAR 2

Just as the seeds or seedlings in a garden need extra protection and care after planting, so too with your dreams and goals planted in the Personal Year 1. The momentum and growth will be slower than in year 1, and you may feel more sensitive than normal. Patience is your watchword, as you tend your plans and move them forward. Be mindful of all of your relationships – at home and at work – and maintain harmony as much as you can. Invite input and advice this year, as others can help and support you in moving toward your dreams. Your focus will be less on yourself and more on others during the 2 Personal Year.

PERSONAL YEAR 3

Self-expression comes to the forefront during Personal Year 3, including speaking your truth, engaging in art or other creative endeavors, and social interactions. You will grow considerably during this year, as you express more of yourself in all arenas of your life. New and exciting people may come into your life, and you will be asked to express your thoughts and beliefs in places you may not have done so before. It can also be a painful year as you work the emotional dimension of the 3 energy – after all, it's not always easy to say what's in your heart! Fun, friends, and frivolity are themes in the 3 year. And it can be a financially positive year too, provided you direct your creativity and self-expression constructively.

PERSONAL YEAR 4

This is a year in which you put systems, structure and a foundation in place for the rest of the cycle. You may need to rein in your creative energy if it has become scattered. But in any event, hard work and dedication are required during a 4 Personal Year. You will need to get organized, be practical, and keep your commitments. Be flexible enough to take advantage of the opportunities that are presented. And if you sense limits and constraints, know that they are part of the 4 Personal Year energy, and will dissipate by the time the 5 year rolls around. If you have considered buying real estate or remodel, this is a good year to do it. Get any insurance, tax or legal issues addressed. And know that the hard work of this year brings great rewards!

PERSONAL YEAR 5

The 5 Personal Year brings change – some expected, some unexpected – and excitement, as well as travel. It is a year to take your "show on the road" and be ready to adapt to changing conditions in the market, your staff, and the business itself. It can be a kind of "high" to ride these waves of change, and the 5 energy also brings temptations in the realm of food, drink, and other addictions. Lucky breaks can come during the 5 year too! Be careful not to put yourself in opposition to the 5 energy by holding tight to what used to work – you're being asked to adapt and change, so let go of the old. Take some calculated risks – they will usually pay off.

PERSONAL YEAR 6

There is a dual energy in the 6 Personal Year. On the one hand you may experience financial progress and the growth of your career or business. And on the other, family and others in need may bring added responsibility, caretaking needs, or feel burdensome. This will require balance! But by understanding this dual energy, and knowing it will not last forever (usually not past the year) makes it easier to bear. Relationships (including business partnerships and staff relationships) can be renewed, or may need to be reexamined.

PERSONAL YEAR 7

Solitude, study and reflection will characterize the 7 Personal Year. After being out marketing yourself in year 5 and caring for others in year 6, year 7 brings a focus on your inner world. Perhaps you will feel a longing to go back to school, engage in extended continuing education, or even learn to meditate or tap into your intuition. You may question your career direction. If you can take a sabbatical, or at least some mini-retreats during this year, it will give you the opportunity you need to go more deeply within yourself to reflect and study. Since your future success is dependent on your inner success and authentic self, the 7 Personal Year gives you a chance to explore who you are and build that foundation on an even more solid ground.

PERSONAL YEAR 8

The 8 Personal Year is harvest time. Everything you touch turns to gold, as you reap the rewards of the past 7 years' activities. Your introspection will give way to more interaction with business associates, customers, and colleagues and will lead to opportunities that can be breathtaking in scope. You will be especially work- and financially-focused in the 8 year. You may find yourself thrust into the role of leader, manager or boss – and you are advised to take it, as you will be successful in that role during the 8 Personal Year! Your mental clarity will have returned and you will likely feel "on fire" with the excitement of your work and its results. However, it is not uncommon for there to be a serious financial loss (e.g., bankruptcy) during an 8 Personal Year. This clears out the energy that would detract from the harvest that is available and prepares you for the next stage of development.

PERSONAL YEAR 9

The end of the cycle is the 9 energy, so this is a year of tying up loose ends, clearing out the old, and making way for the new. It can be compared to the farmer plowing the old crop's stubble under to till the ground for the new crop. Any clutter must be cleared away, such as accumulated items in a garage or attic, old files or records, or excess body weight. Any relationships that are no longer in synch with who you are – and who you are becoming – must be surrendered too. Contributing to charitable causes is also advisable in a 9 year, and the more you give the more you tend to earn. You may also feel drawn to enjoy music, the arts, and other creative activities during the 9 Personal Year. Bring closure to all that needs it, so that no unnecessary burdens, relationships or energy are brought into the new cycle when it begins next year.

PERSONAL MONTHS

Within each year, there will be a mini-cycle of personal months following this same sequence. By knowing both the Personal Year and Personal Month, you can properly sequence your business activities for best results. And if you have missed the mark on fulfilling the energy of the last Personal Year with a specific energy or number, you can revisit that number when it appears as a Personal Month and complete the work.

HOW TO CALCULATE YOUR PERSONAL MONTH

To calculate your Personal Month, you simply add the number of your Personal Year to the Universal Month.

For example, if it is April (the fourth month of the year), and you are in a Personal Year 8, you add 4 to 8 to get 12; 1 + 2 = 3 so April is a 3 month for you.

The meaning of each of the Personal Months is the same, on a smaller scale, as the Personal Years listed above.

To calculate your Personal Day, just add your Personal Month to the calendar day – so 12th of the month with an 8 life path = 1 Personal Day. When your Personal Day number matches either your Life Path number or your Expression number, pay special attention – these days will have special impact and significance.

RECOMMENDED BUSINESS ACTIVITIES BY PERSONAL YEAR/ MONTH

Following is a planning guide outlining representative recommended activities to perform in each of the 9 Personal Years or Personal Months:

Business tasks to do in Personal Year or Month 1: start a business, launch a new program or product, hire new staff, introduce a new brand

Business tasks to do in Personal Year or Month 2: tend the results of the activities in Personal Year/Month 1 to ensure they grow, provide outstanding customer service, do a customer survey, visit customers and dialog with them about their needs

Business tasks to do in Personal Year or Month 3: bring a more creative approach to your marketing or web site, hone your company message to fully express the business mission and philosophy, have a company picnic or a customer appreciation party

Business tasks to do in Personal Year or Month 4: establish policies, procedures, structures and protocols for all aspects of your business, create operations manuals, complete all legal documentation for corporate entities and transactions, and acquire software or web-based systems to manage business functions, buy or rent new space for the business, get insurance in place, address any tax issues

Business tasks to do in Personal Year or Month 5: make any needed changes to staff or processes to be more effective, enjoy the exciting new people that you encounter and the travel opportunities, ride the wave of any market changes to which you can quickly respond with products or services, get out in the marketplace and do public relations and promotion

Business tasks to do in Personal Year or Month 6: take outstanding care of your tribe or market by nurturing them and drawing them together, balance any added family responsibilities with work, expect positive financial results during the 6 year/month, take responsibility for all aspects of your business and its effects on others, do community or charitable outreach

Business tasks to do in Personal Year or Month 7: study to become an expert in your field – or to broaden your knowledge, heed any intuitive hunches that come to you during this period, carve out time for personal retreats or planning retreats to reflect on where you have been and where you are going

Business tasks to do in Personal Year or Month 8: step you marketing and sales, expand into new markets, enter joint ventures, and any other activities that will activate and leverage the favorable energies for money, business and power

Business tasks to do in Personal Year or Month 9: close a business, clean out files, purge outdated materials, update and organize systems

I trust that you have enjoyed this quick tour through the world of Business Numerology and how to create fulfillment and wealth through aligning your business and its activities with the numerology profile of you, any co-owners, and the cycles of business and life. Have fun applying it!

ABOUT MARCIA BENCH

Marcia Bench is the world's #1 Business Numerologist, a spiritual business coach, Energy Realignment specialist, best-selling author and professional speaker. She has more than 25 years' experience coaching, training, and speaking to entrepreneurs and professional groups. She is the author of 25 books and has been coaching and consulting both individual and corporate clients since 1986. Her companies include Your Divine Gifts http://www.yourdivinegifts.com, and Career Coach Institute, http://www.careercoachinstitute.com, as well as other coaching companies.

A former attorney, Marcia's books include *Become an Inspirational Thought Leader, The Tao of Entrepreneurship: 52 Lessons in Applying Spiritual Principles to Business Ownership,* and *Career Coaching: An Insider's Guide.*

Marcia has been a featured speaker/trainer at hundreds of local, regional and national conferences, as well as on hundreds of teleclasses and guest appearances on numerous television and radio programs. Her mission is to help individuals increase their sense of enjoyment and meaning in their work.

Marcia's coaching experience includes work with managers and executives from Fortune 500 firms in a variety of industries as well as dozens of business owners, professionals, and military officers entering the civilian workforce.

Prior to entering the coaching industry, Marcia was Senior Vice President in a dot-com career management firm for 4 years, and previously spent 10 years as President of New Work Directions, a business and consulting firm she founded. Ms. Bench developed her expertise in business start-up and management in part through her 4 years as a practicing attorney specializing in business and employment issues.

Marcia's education includes a Juris Doctorate from Northwestern School of Law of Lewis & Clark College and a Bachelor of Science in Psychology from Western Oregon University. In addition, she is a Certified Career Management Practitioner through the International Board of Career Management Certification, a Certified Business Coach, a Certified Teleader and Master Certified Career Coach.

Marcia Bench Enterprises, LLC
29030 SW Town Ctr Lp E #202-444
Wilsonville, OR 97070
www.yourdivinegifts.com

RECOMMENDED PROGRAMS AND PRODUCTS BY MARCIA BENCH

BUSINESS NUMEROLOGY READINGS

After reading the highlights of numerology in this guidebook, you may now be curious to have your own personal reading with Marcia or one of her staff! Readings can address your Soul's Blueprint (core numbers interpretation), your Future Forecast (for the next 3 years), or a Business Relationship Compatibility Reading before you enter into a partnership or hire a team member. Contact info@yourdivinegifts. com or see our Readings page at http://www.yourdivinegifts.com for details.

CERTIFIED BUSINESS NUMEROLOGIST™ TRAINING

Want to become a professional Certified Business Numerologist™ and make your living doing readings, coaching and workshops using numerology? Our 12-module training gets you qualified in just weeks! Get the details at http://www.certifiedbusinessnumerologist. com

CAREER COACH TRAINING AND CERTIFICATION

Marcia's blended learning approach to learning career coaching and getting certified have changed the lives of hundreds of people worldwide. If you want to learn coaching skills and develop career design and job search mechanics expertise – as well as practice coaching in real time and get feedback – you will want to explore our career coach training. You will join a worldwide community of coaches with a similar passion for career coaching and the same fundamental approach. Training is delivered online or, on occasion, in person or via live teleclass, and is also available for corporate groups. Visit http://www.careercoachinstitute.com for details.

BOOKS, CD'S, AND OTHER PRODUCTS

Marcia's other 24 books and many information products are available at her online store at http://www.yourdivinegifts.com as well as her Amazon Author Page here: http://www.amazon.com/Marcia-Bench/e/B001KJ1UE0

BUSINESS BUILDING SUPPORT AND TRAINING

Marcia has used sound principles of business building to grow to where she is today. In addition to this book, she offers other training and mentoring programs to help coaches and infopreneurs build their businesses. See http://www.yourdivinegifts.com for details.

CORPORATE NUMEROLOGY SERVICES

Marcia's companies also offer retainer services for companies who want ongoing mentoring and insights on both numerology and their marketing strategy. Contact info@yourdivinegifts.com for details.

LIVE EVENTS AND SPEAKING ENGAGEMENTS

Marcia periodically offers live training events, sacred site travel and retreats for committed entrepreneurs and professionals. To be notified of upcoming events, register to receive Marcia's ezine, Inspire!, at http://www.yourdivinegifts.com. And to hire Marcia to speak at your event or for a media interview, contact info@yourdivinegifts.com or visit http://www.yourdivinegifts.com

Don't see what you're looking for? Contact our customer service team at 503-308-8179 or email us at info@yourdivinegifts.com. We are here to support your success!